THE PHOTO-LIBR

George Reid

River Thames

in the late Twenties & early Thirties

Edited by Mike Seaborne
Text by Chris Ellmers

NISHEN

Editorial Notice

All the pictures shown in this book are from the collection of the Museum of London. The publisher would like to thank Mike Seaborne, Curator of the Museum's Historic Photographs Collection.
New prints for reproduction were made from copy negatives of the original prints. The pictures are reproduced by permission of the Reid Archive Collection.

The Photo-Library is being edited by Colin Osman and Dirk Nishen

Front Cover:
The Houses of Parliament, photographed from east of Lambeth Pier. Launches, tugs, a sailing barge and moored coal lighters provided much of interest for the spectator.

Back Cover:
The cobbled causeway under Southwark Bridge, looking towards Cannon Street Railway Bridge. At low tide the river foreshore was a haven for children. On the right are Borax Wharf, Southwark Wharf, Bridge Wharf and Ceylon Wharf, with the Dutch auxiliary coaster, *›Stella‹*, alongside.

The publisher will be pleased to send further information on the titles available in his current programme, a selection of which you will find on the concluding page of this volume. Please send a postcard to the adress given below.

Typesetting: Nishen/Lübecker Fotosatz, using the Linotype Walbaum type-face
Lithographs: O.R.T. Kirchner + Graser, D-Berlin
Printing: H.Heenemann, D-Berlin
Binding: H.Hensch, D-Berlin
The publisher wishes to thank all parties involved

ISBN 1 85378 101 0

George Reid's Views of the River Thames

During the 1920s and 1930s, the London River was an exciting and ever changing theatre: its stage, the tideway; its backdrop, the bridges, wharves and warehouses; its players, the ships, tugs and barges and their crews; its audience, a vast number of Londoners and visitors.

In the late 1920s and 1930s, when George Reid took his series of photographs of the Thames, London was still the greatest port in the world. With a population of over four million, London was the trading centre of the largest empire the world had ever seen. Through this port, each year, passed some 35 million tons of import and export cargoes, worth some £ 700 million. These cargoes were carried by a huge number of ocean going ships, which made some 40,000 visits, besides coasters, which made a further 14,000 trips. In addition, 270,000 passengers, to and from overseas, also passed through the port. London's seven major dock systems – operated by the Port of London Authority – contained over 700 acres of man-made water and there were some 1,700 working wharves between Brentford, upstream, and Gravesend, downriver. Around 100,000 dockers, stevedores, lightermen, sailors and ancillary workers depended directly upon the Port of London for their livelihood.

George Reid's view of the port, however, is not that of the great dock systems – with their endless expanses of water, massive warehouses, large cargo ships and smart liners – guarded, as they were, by tall dock walls and policemen. Rather, it is the view of port activities on a part of the busy tideway, which any Londoner could have enjoyed and wondered at. Concentrating on the area between Tower Bridge and Vauxhall Bridge, Reid used his considerable technical and artistic abilities to produce a superb series of photographs which record events as diverse as sunrise over Tower Bridge and the loading of rubbish barges. One focus, in particular, was on the more humble craft of London's River. Recorded by his lens are just some of the 10.000 lighters and 1000 sailing barges which worked at everything from transporting cargoes, upriver, from the lower docks, to carrying away the city's refuse. Traditional ship portraiture, fortunately, held no attraction for him. There is much, too, of human interest in his photographs – port workers and port watchers, alike, were candidly preserved for posterity.

We owe George Reid a great deal of gratitude for having turned his camera lens to some of the less well recorded wharves and warehouses, for only a handful now survive. The upheavals of the war years, the gradual closure of the upriver docks and river wharves, from the late 1960s, and large scale re-developments, have all taken their toll. Likewise, ships and coasters no longer visit the sites recorded by Reid, there are no sailing barges left in trade and most of London's once-proud fleet of lighters have been broken up.

Above all, Reid's photographs prompt both an interest in themselves, as a contemporary record, and a desire to discover what has since become of some of the localities. It is salutary, for instance, to learn that the National Theatre, on the South Bank, is built on the sites of a flour mill, a gravel wharf, a whisky wharf and the City Corporation's rubbish wharf. Never again will its river front echo to the sound of wind in the rigging of moored sailing barges, the clanging of cranes and lighters, the whistles of passing steam tugs and the shouts of bargemen. Now there was theatre!

Chris Ellmers

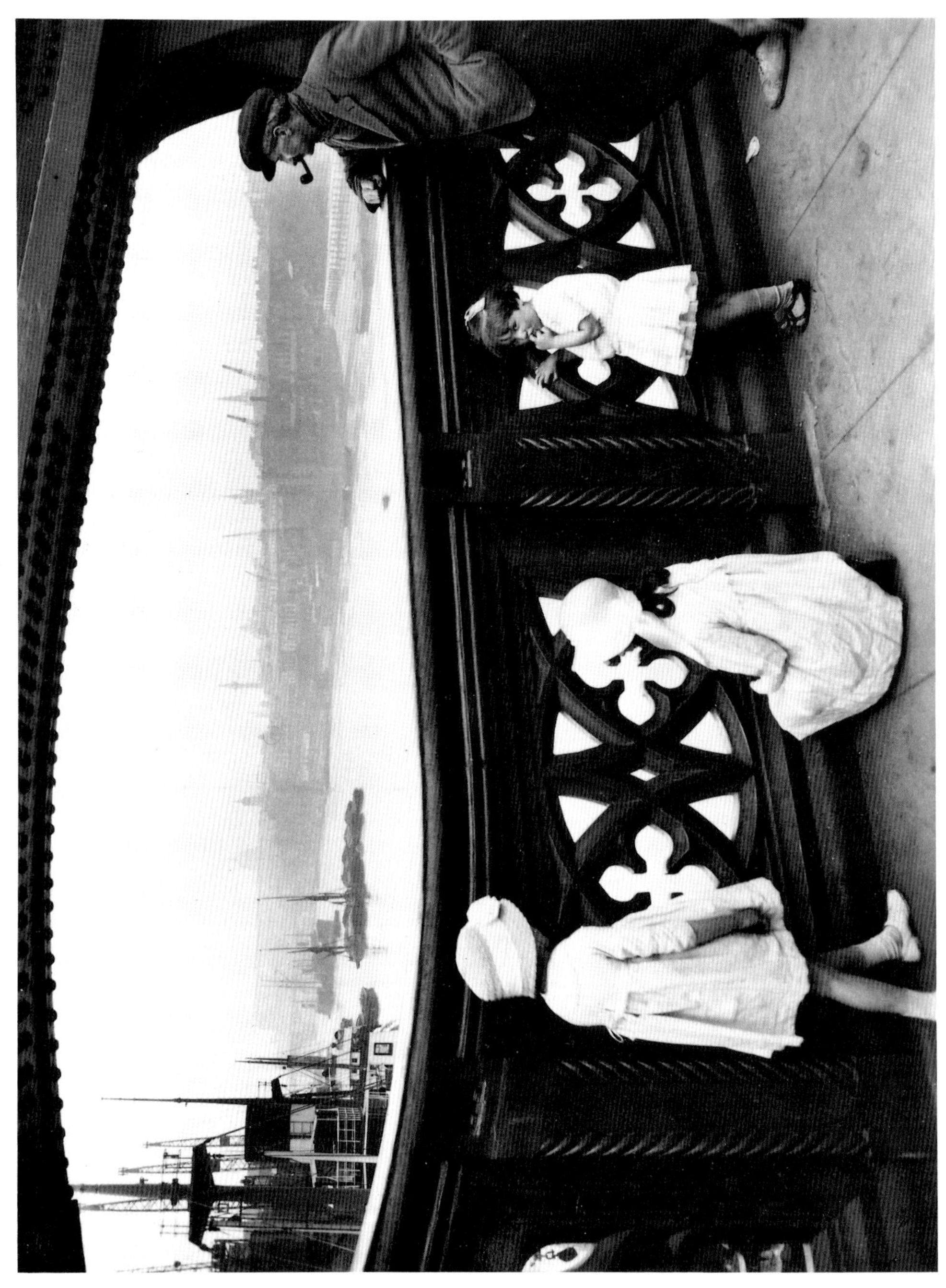

London's many bridges offered the best peepshow of the busy port at work. Here three little girls are looking across the Upper Pool, from the south side of Tower Bridge, towards London Bridge. While the girls are dressed in their summer, ›Sunday best‹, clothes, the man is well-wrapped against the river's breeze.

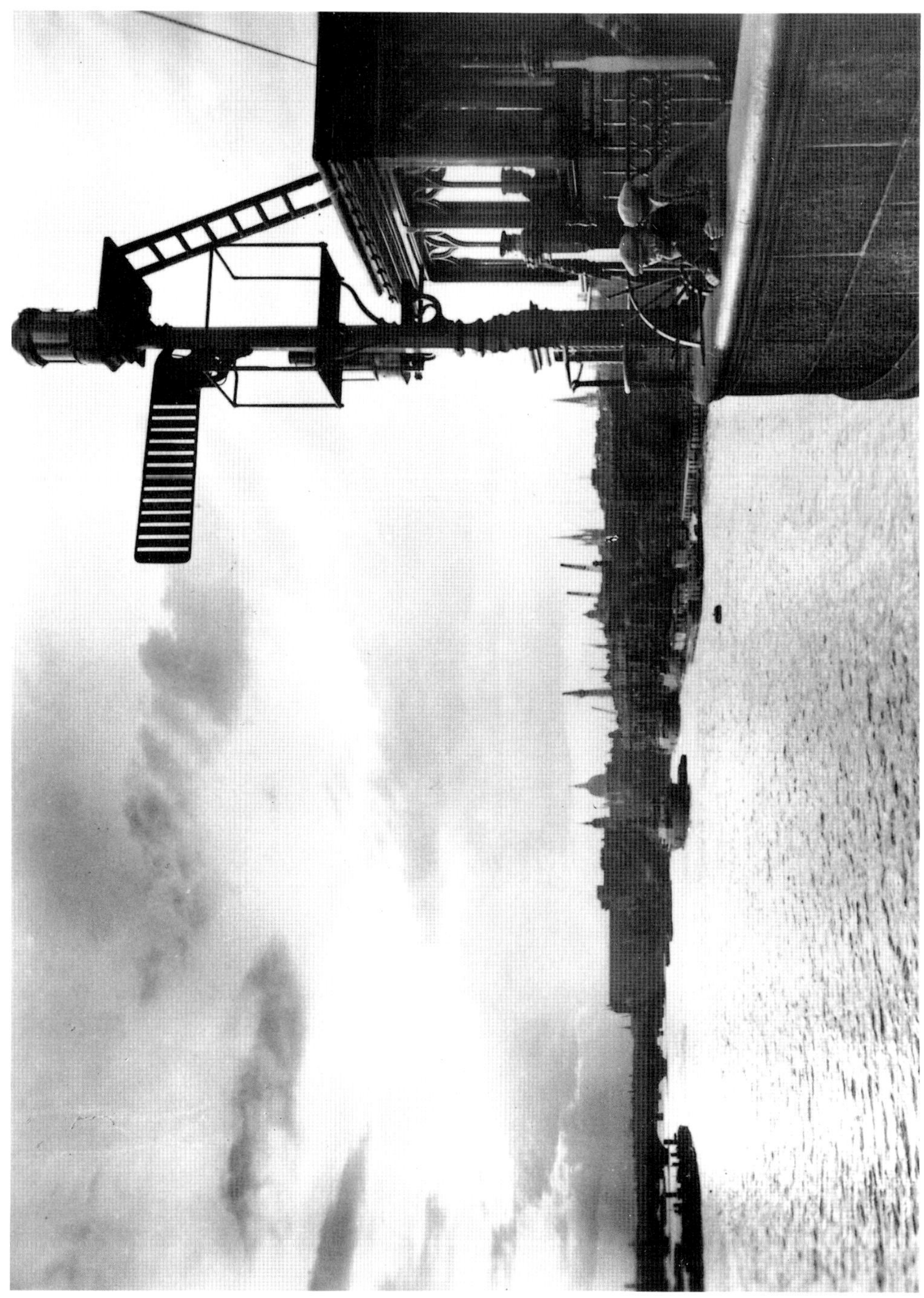

Sunset over the north shore, of the Upper Pool, seen from Tower Bridge (1894). The signal lamps and semaphore helped guide ships through the lifting bascules of the bridge, operated from the control box on the right.

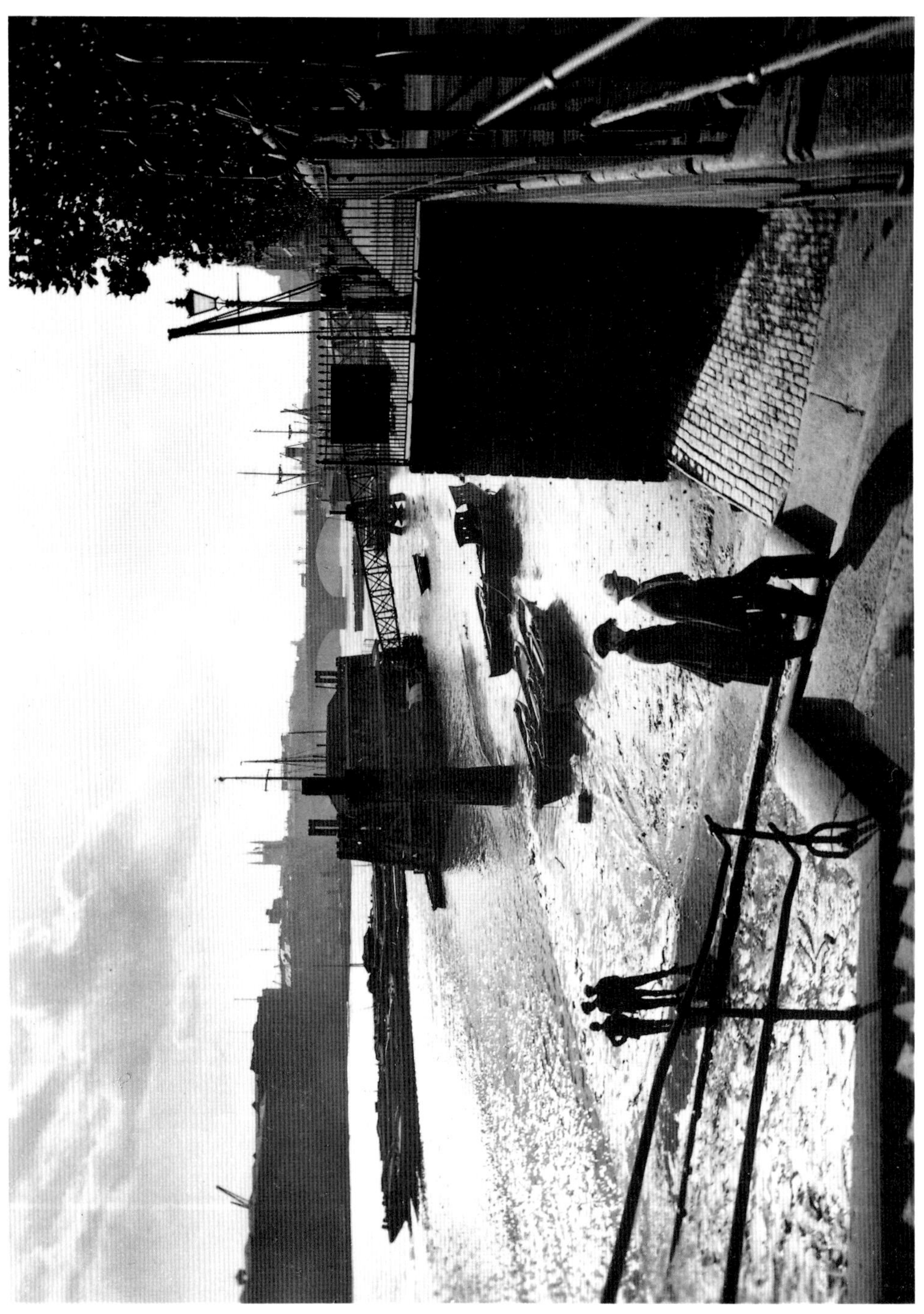

The Upper Pool, looking south-west, from Lower Custom House Stairs. The riverfront was lined with stairs and causeways, used by watermen to ferry river workers and passengers in their skiffs, some of which appear in the foreground. The floating pier, ›*HMS Harpy*‹, belonged to the Custom House.

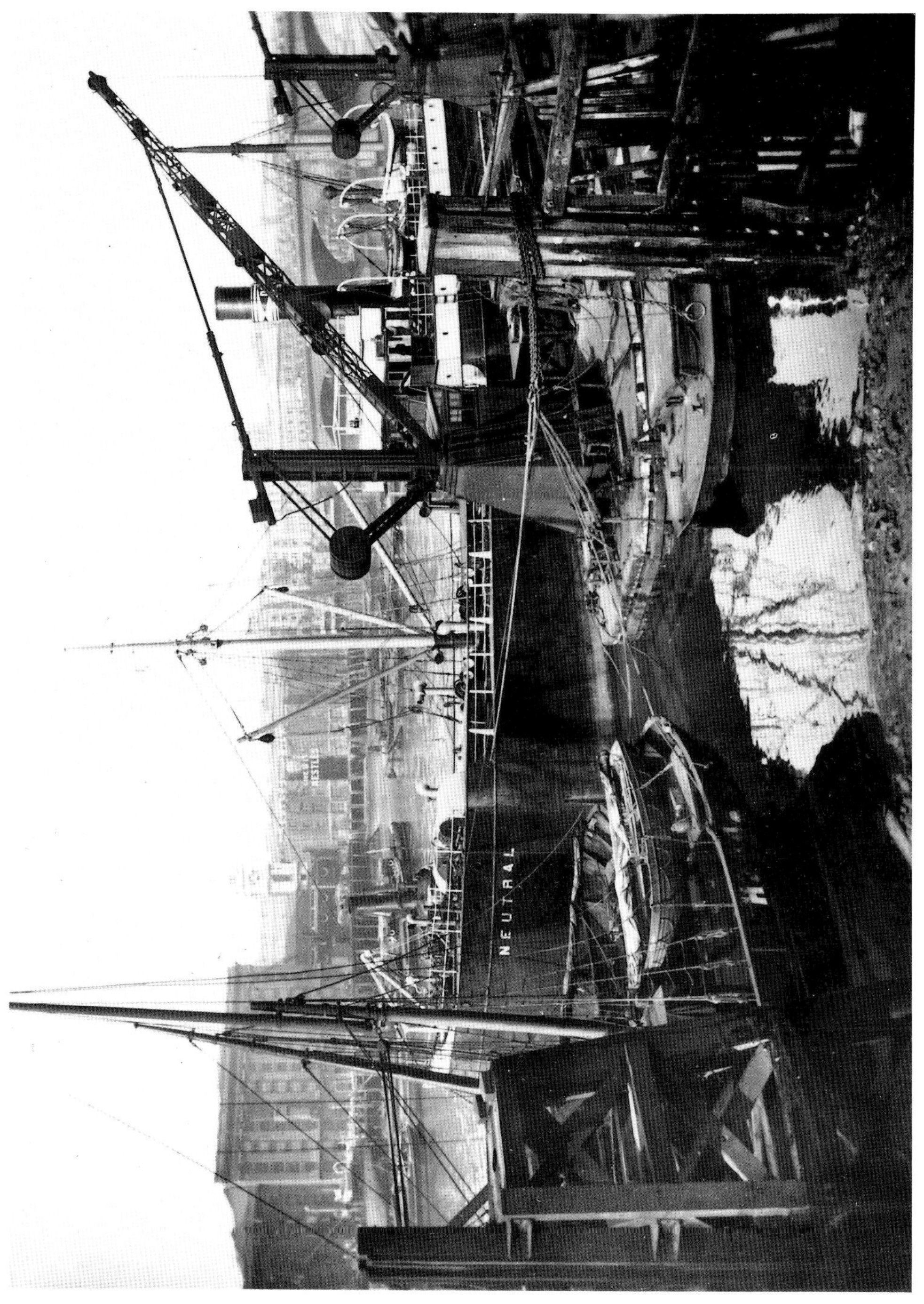

A busy scene of Custom House Quay, looking towards Hay's Wharf and London Bridge. The ›*Neutral*‹, a German owned general cargo steamer, built in 1894, has come up through Tower Bridge. On the jetty can be seen two hydraulic cranes.

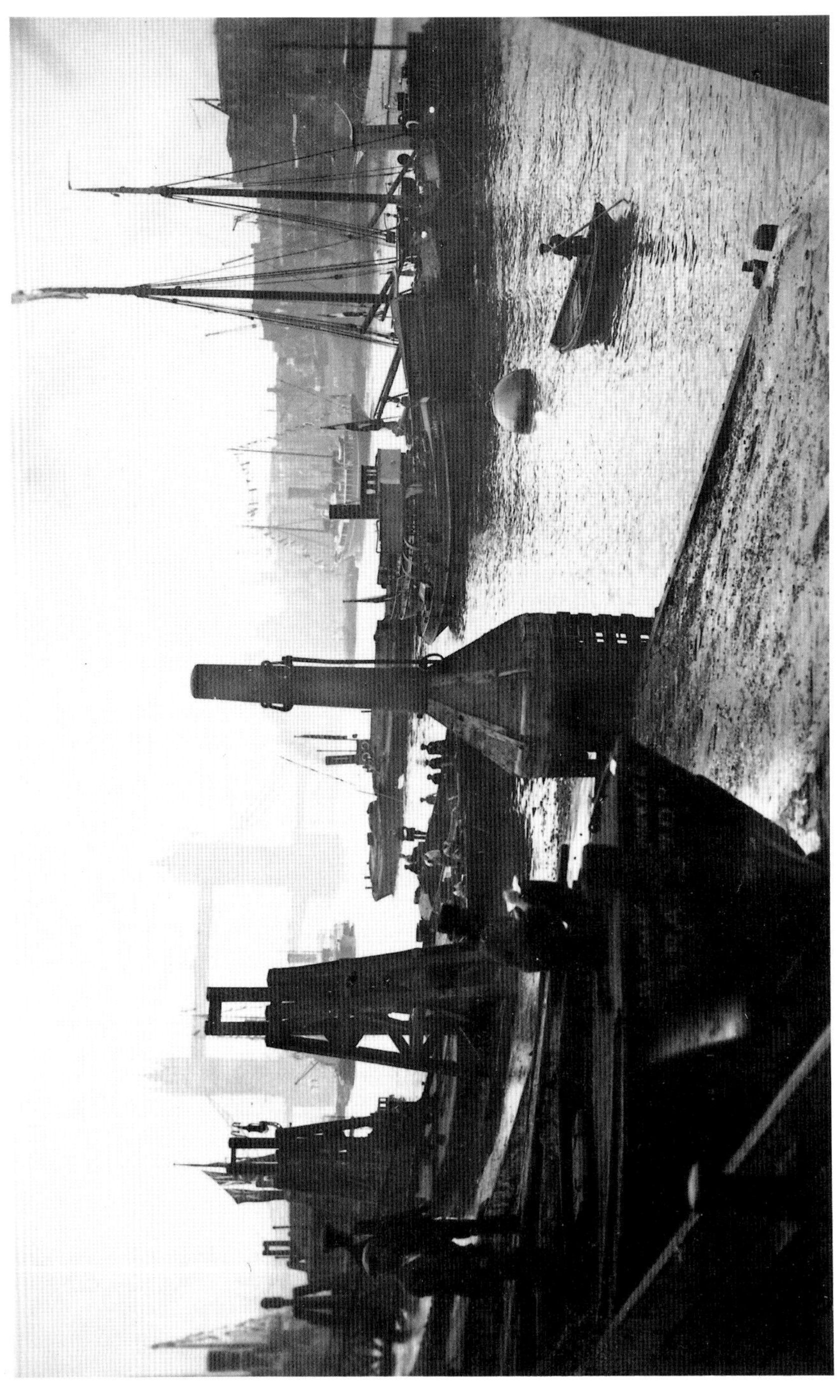

Billingsgate Fish Market jetty, looking towards Tower Bridge. During the 1920s, fish was still brought here, by fast steam carriers, from the North Sea. White smocked fish porters can be seen on the lighter next to the jetty. The two rigged vessels are Dutch eel schuyts.

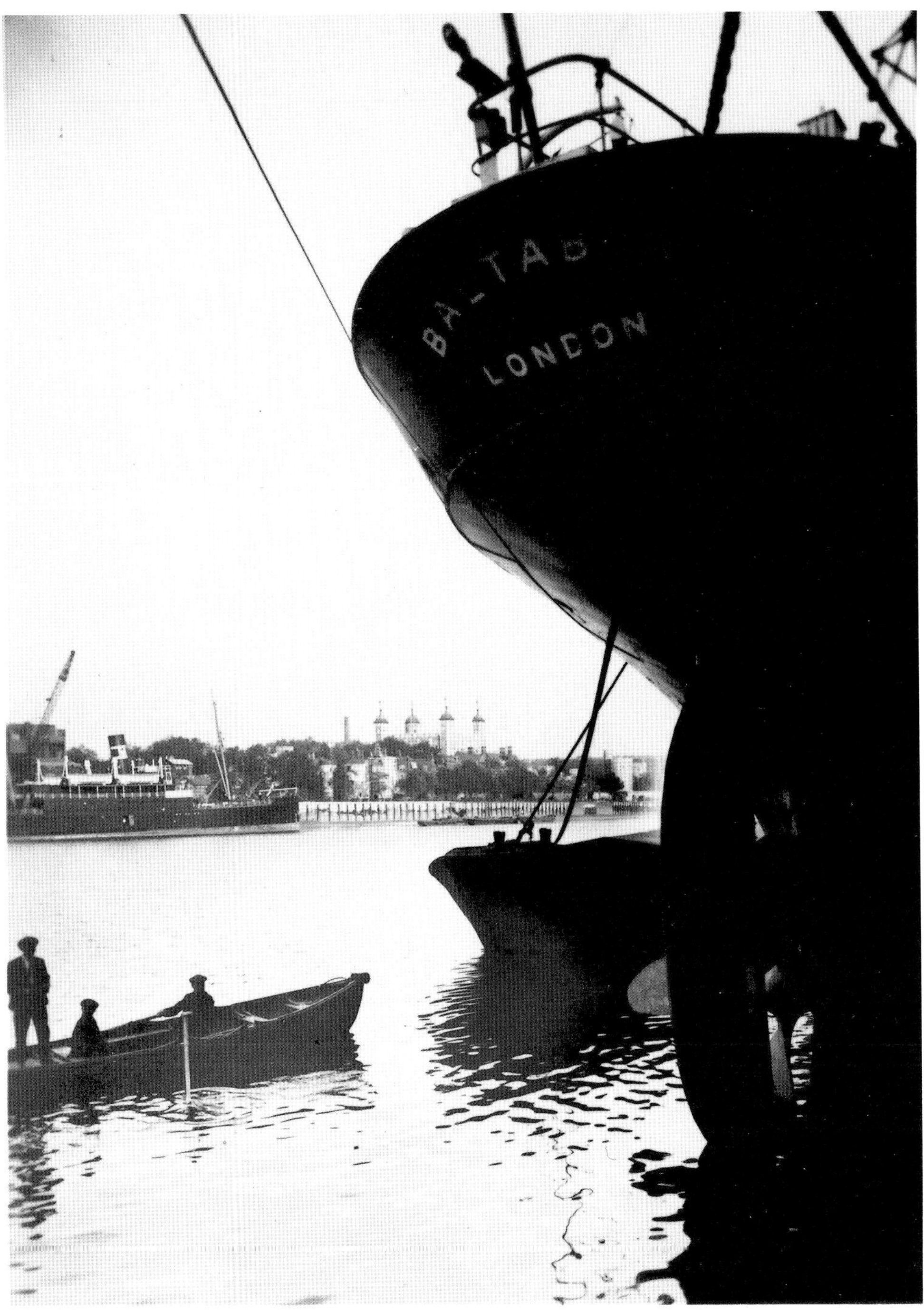

The Upper Pool, looking towards Brewer's Quay and the Tower of London. A waterman's skiff is about to pass the stern of the ›*Baltabor*‹, owned by the United Baltic Corporation, which has carried dairy produce to the Hay's Wharf group of warehouses.

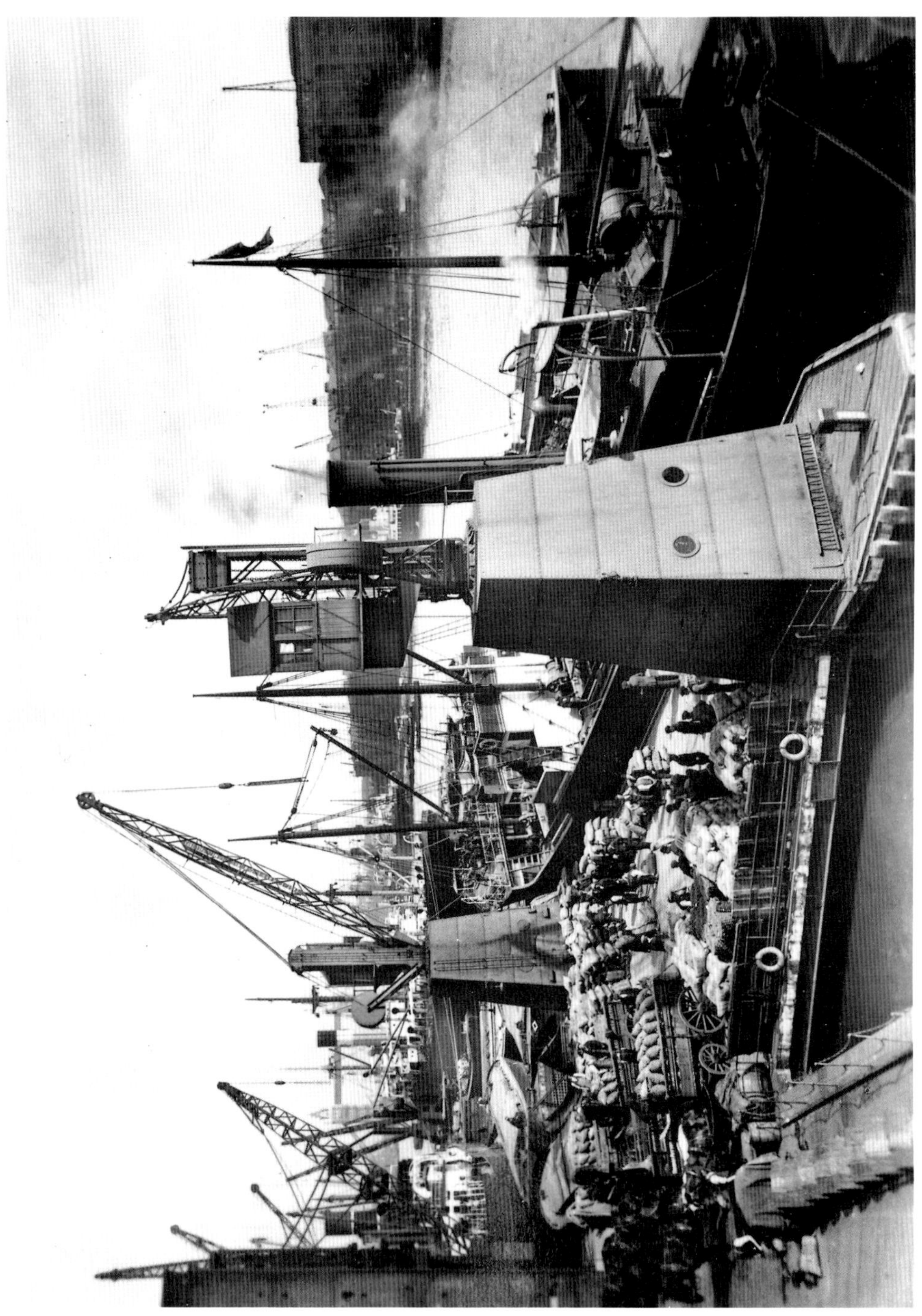

The hustle and bustle of Fresh Wharf, seen from the north side of London Bridge, with a steamer being discharged by hydraulic cranes and her own derricks. This busy wharf mainly handled canned goods, fresh fruit and vegetables, sacks of which are being loaded onto waiting carts, for market.

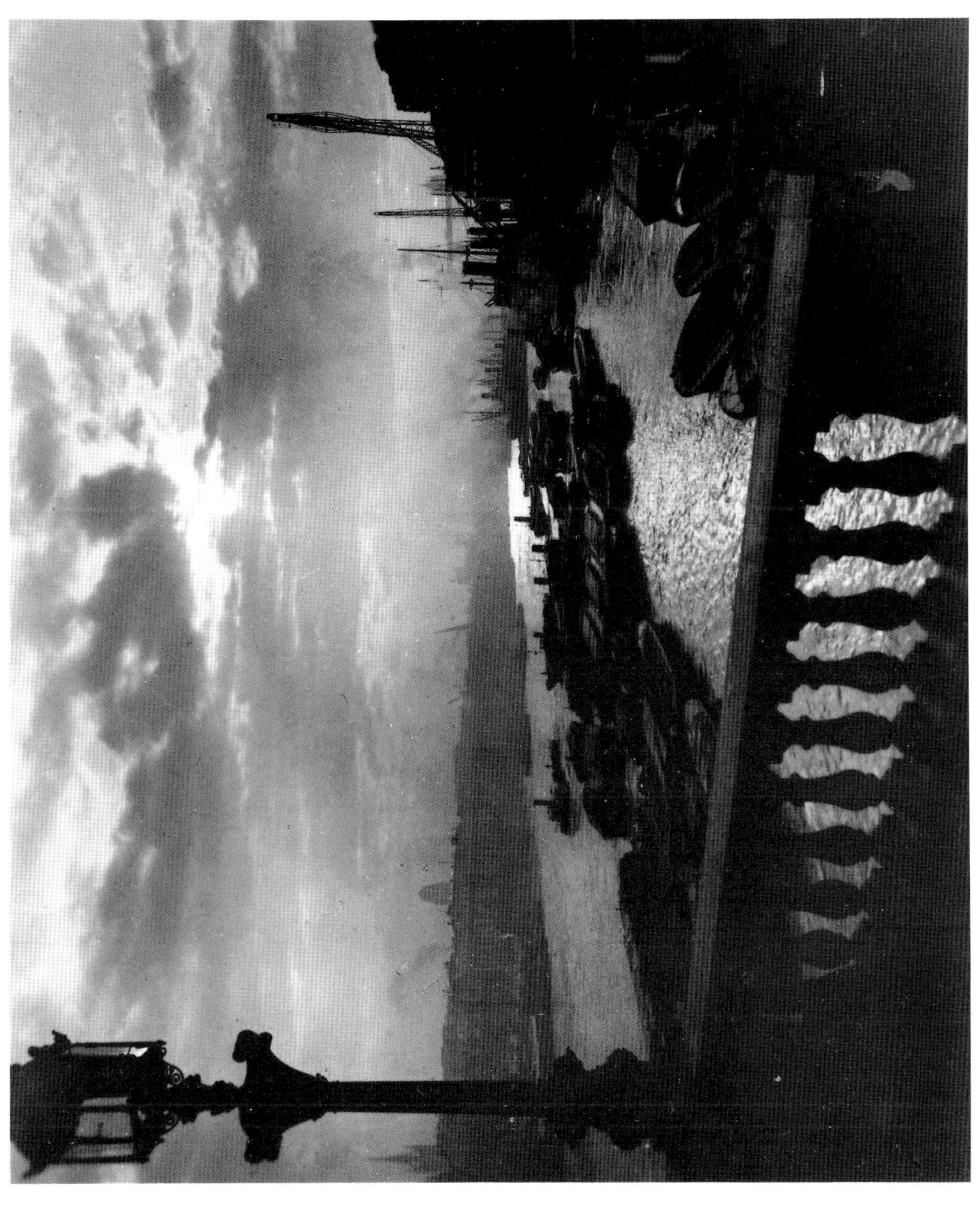

Sunrise over the Upper Pool, from London Bridge, looking towards Tower Bridge. The warehouses on the south bank, occupied by the Hay's Wharf group, were known as ›London's Larder‹, from their handling of dairy produce, tea, coffee and other foodstuffs.

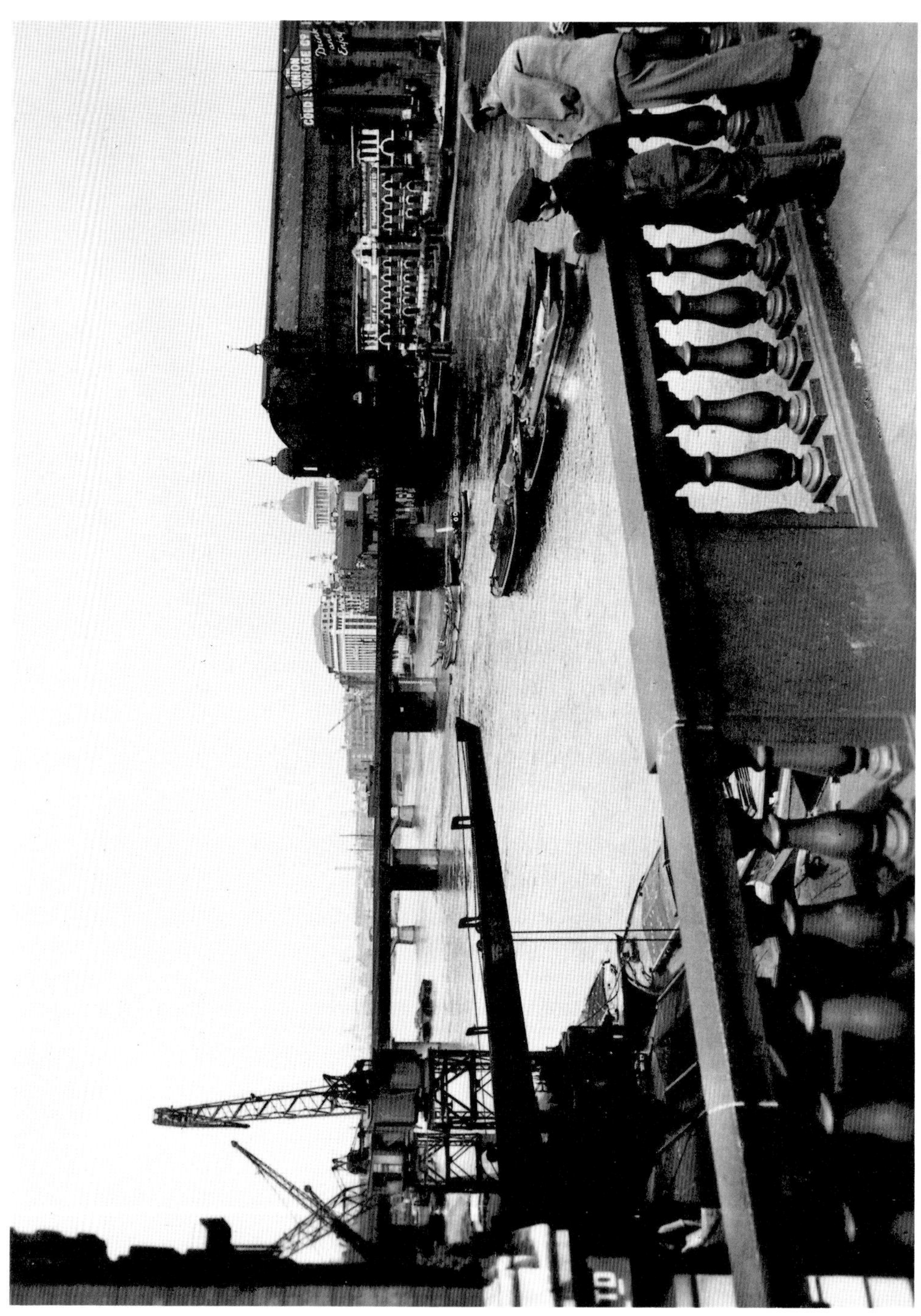

A Post Office telegram boy, and a man with his arm in a sling, look down from old London Bridge (1831–1971) onto barges, whose cargoes of foodstuffs are being discharged at Hibernia Wharves, belonging to the Hay's Wharf group.

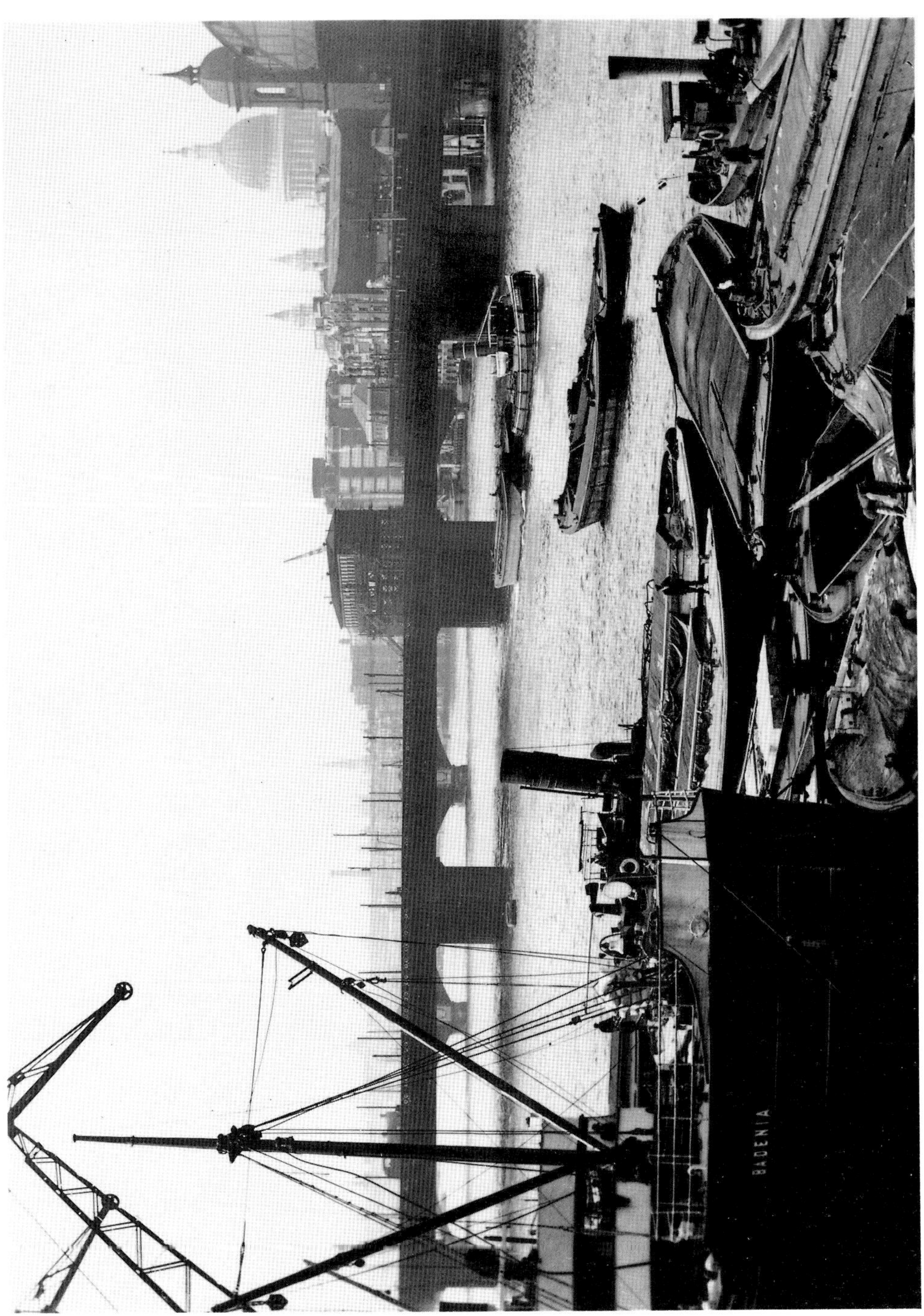

A German steam coaster, the ›*Badenia*‹, tugs and lighters lying at Hibernia Wharves. Lighters not only brought foodstuffs here, from the lower docks, but also received cargoes, from coasters, for delivery further up-river. On two of the barges can be seen the large ›sweeps‹, or oars, used to propel these craft, when tugs were not being used.

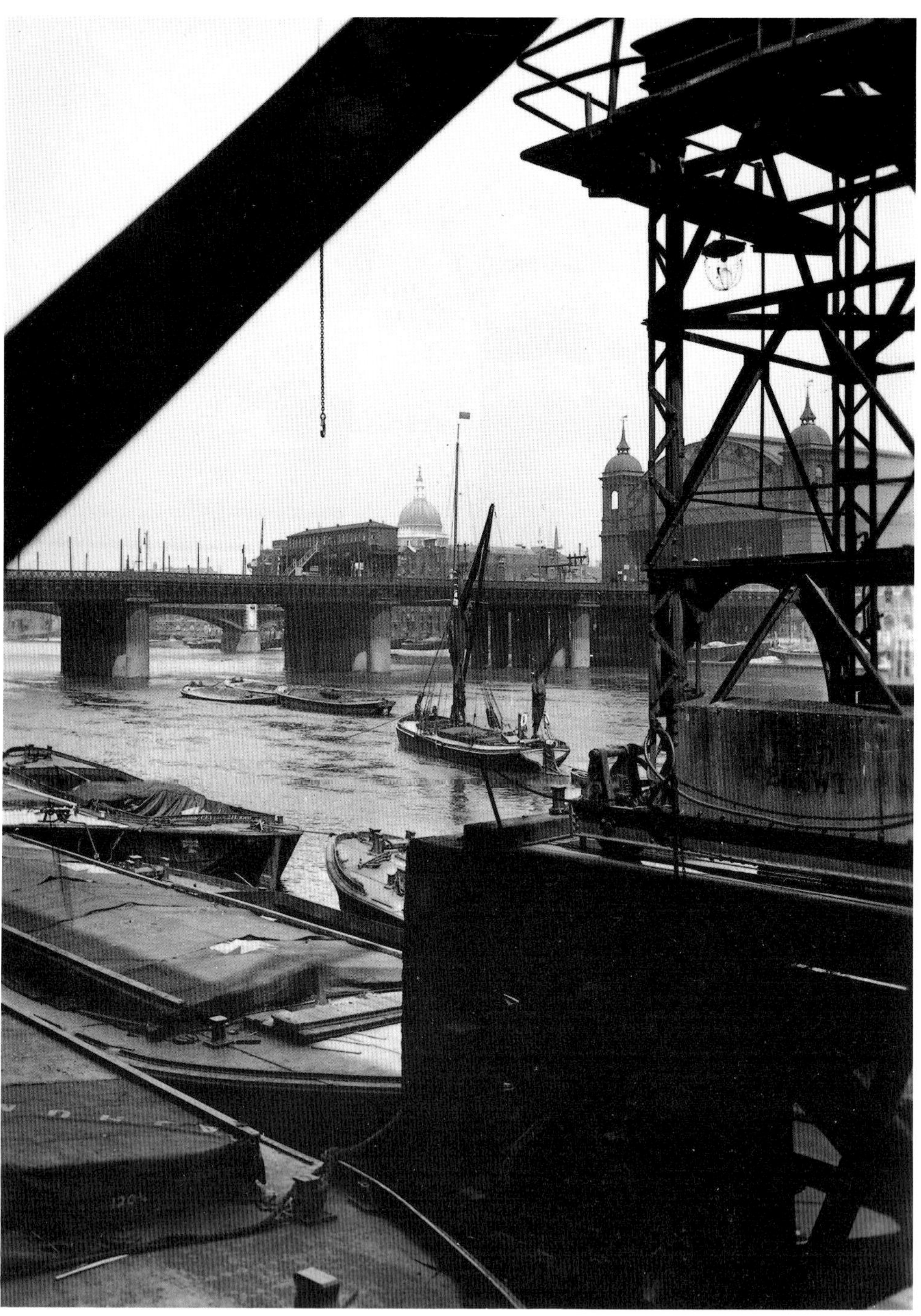

A view from the jetty at Hibernia Wharves, with the legs of one of its large electric quayside cranes, on the right. In the distance can be seen Cannon Street Railway Bridge and Station (opened 1866), with the dome of St Paul's Cathedral behind.

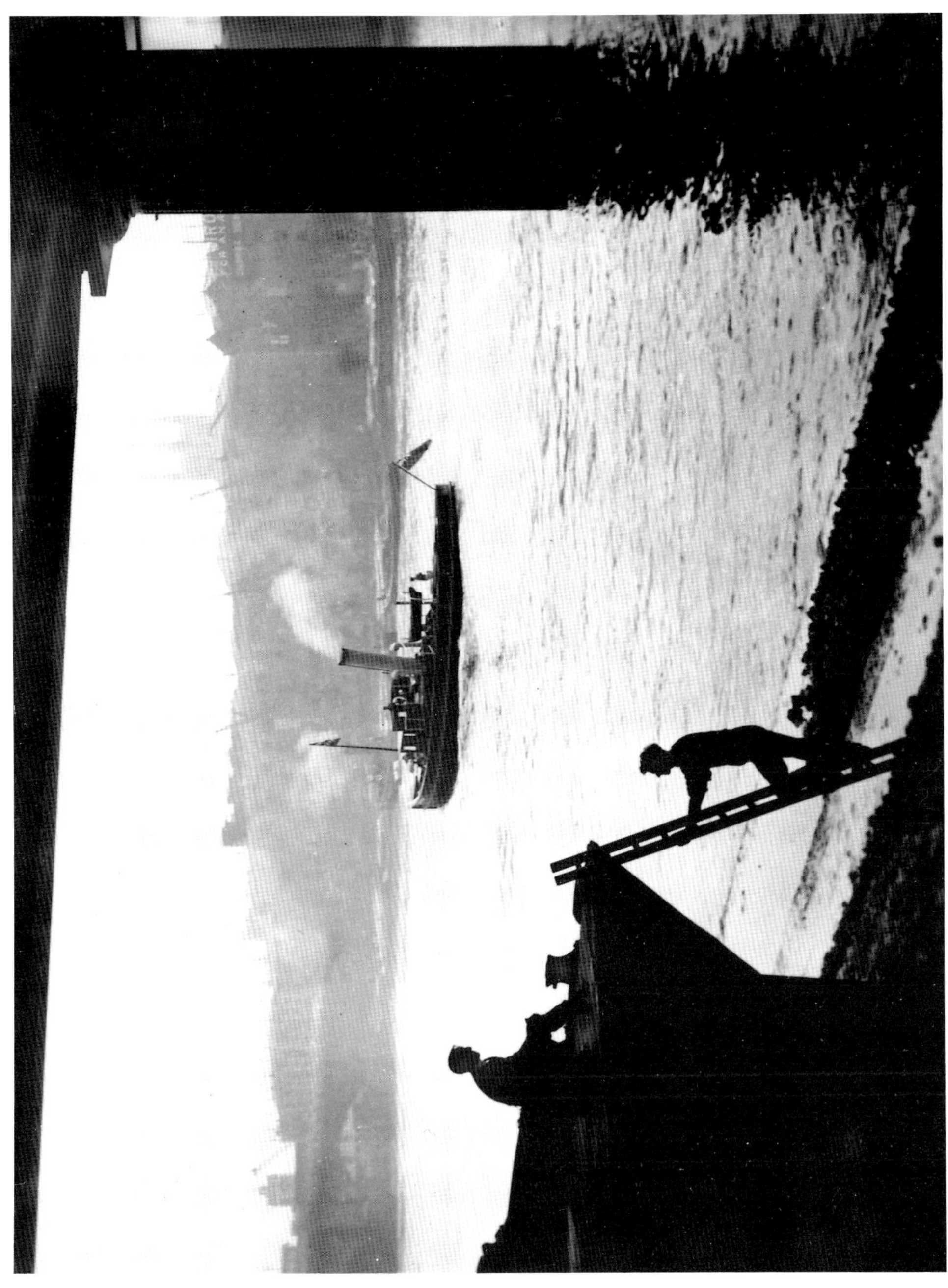

An early morning view of Hibernia Wharves, Southwark Cathedral and London Bridge, seen from the north shore, beneath Cannon Street Railway Bridge. A Port of London Authority steam launch is bound downriver.

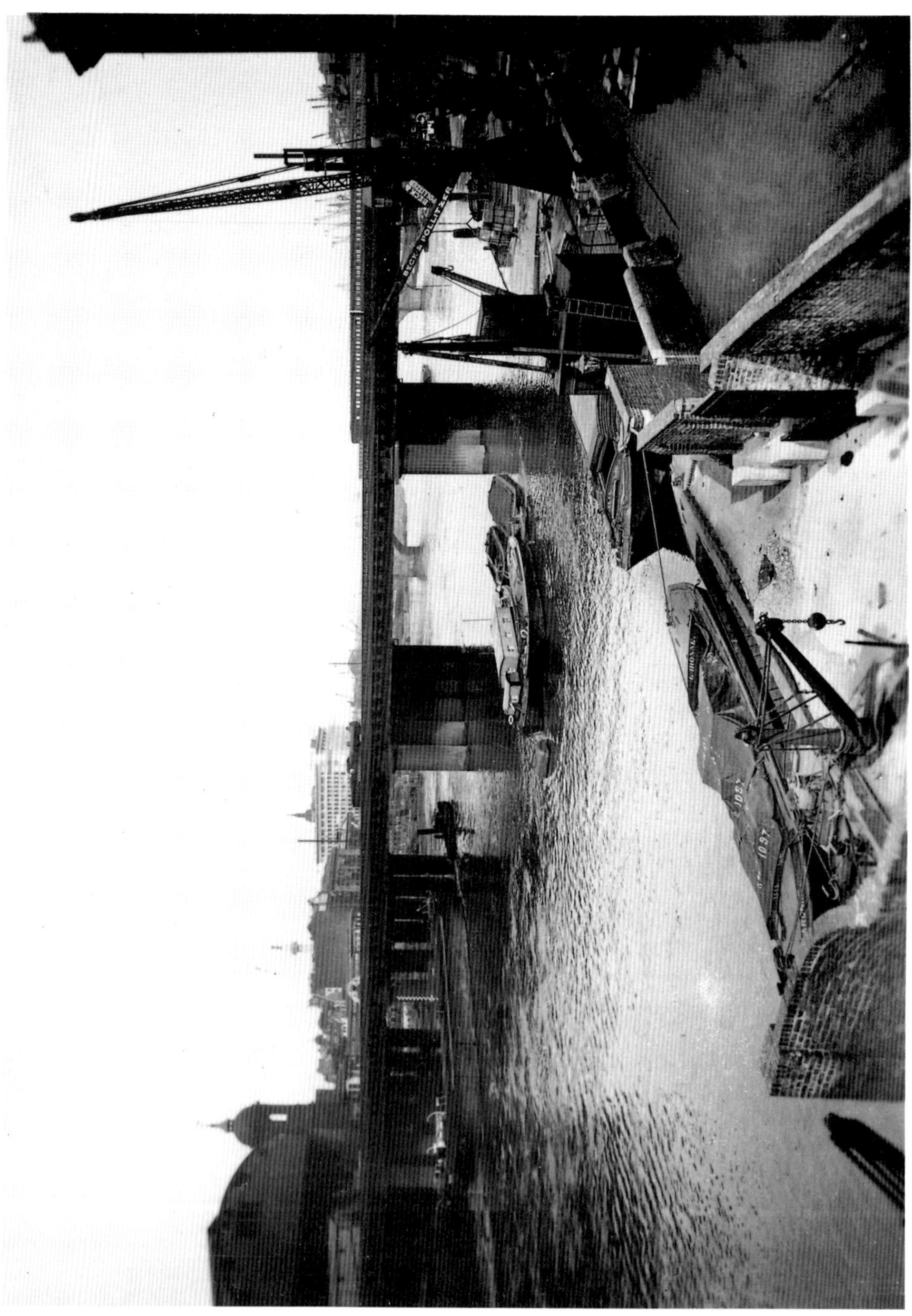

The Bankside riverfront, seen from Southwark Bridge. A carling hatch lighter is being unloaded, by hydraulic cranes, alongside Beck and Pollitzer's Southwark Wharf. This wharf handled general cargoes, including paper, canned goods and mattings.

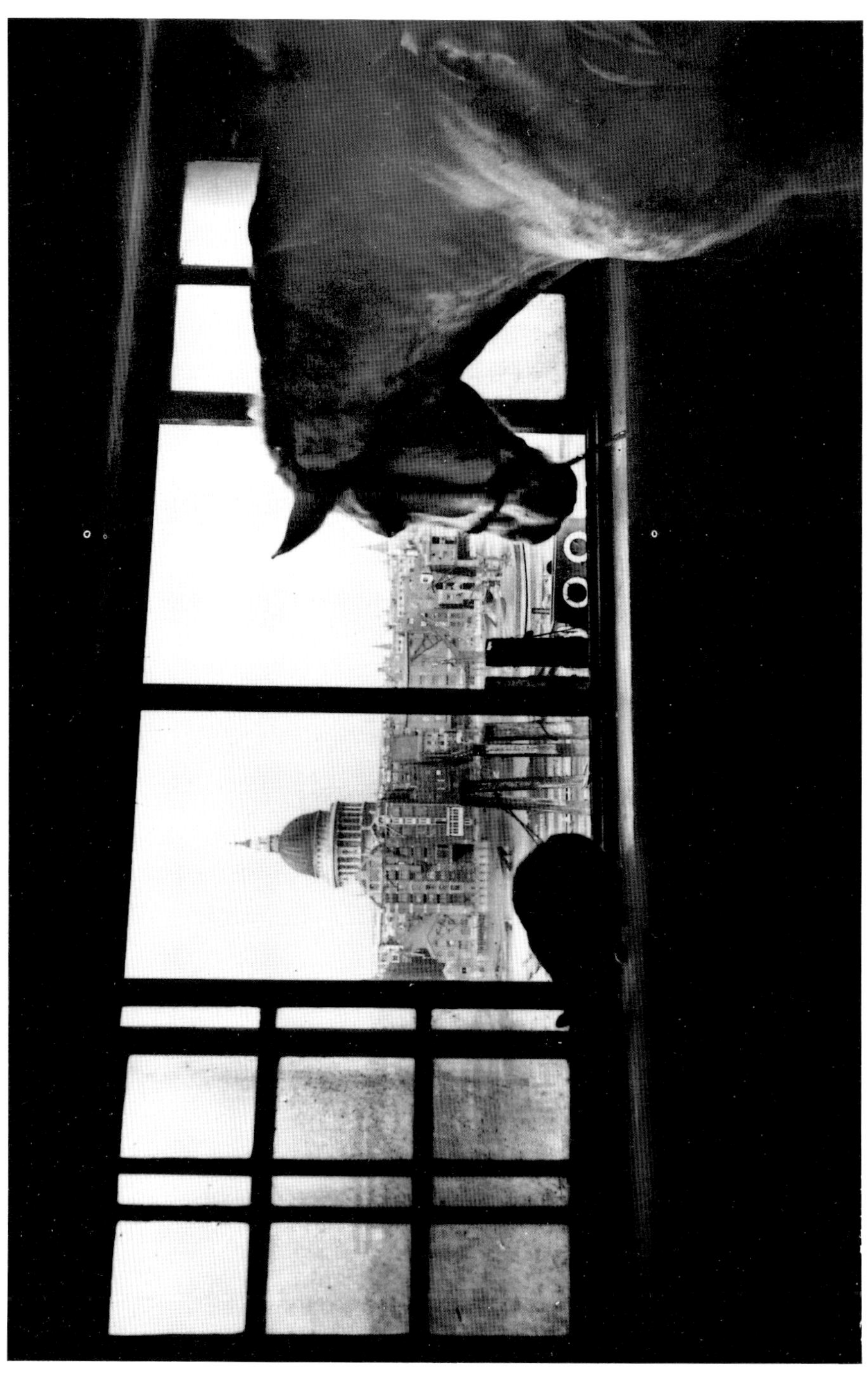

View of the city riverfront, dominated by St Paul's Cathedral, taken from a multi-storey stable building, close to Southwark Bridge. The horse appears to be enjoying the scene!

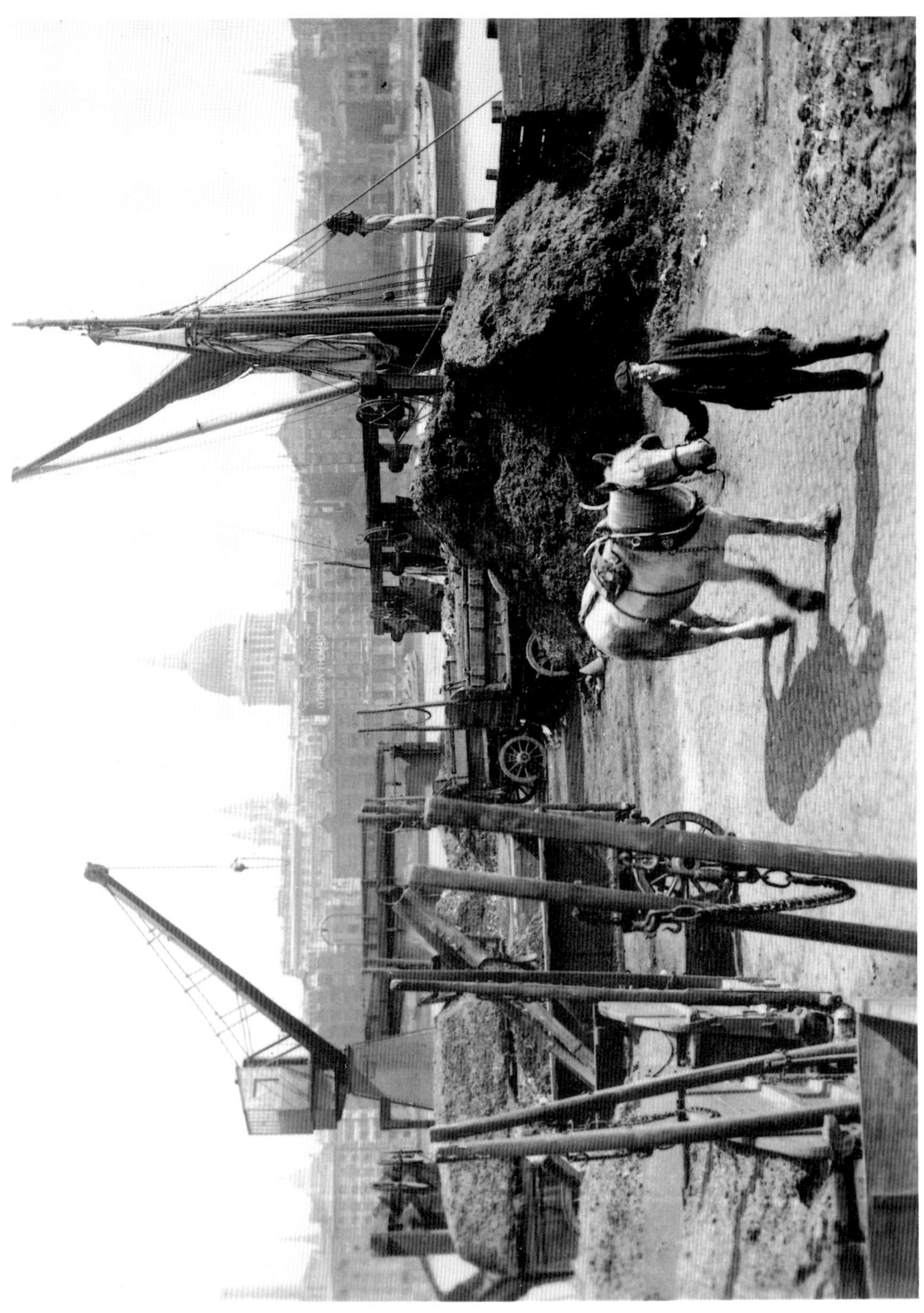

Southwark Corporation's rubbish depot, Greenmoor Wharf, Bankside. Refuse – which here appears to be mainly horse dung – was brought in by cart and loaded into barges, by chutes and hydraulic crane. The wharves and warehouses of the City waterfront appear in the background.

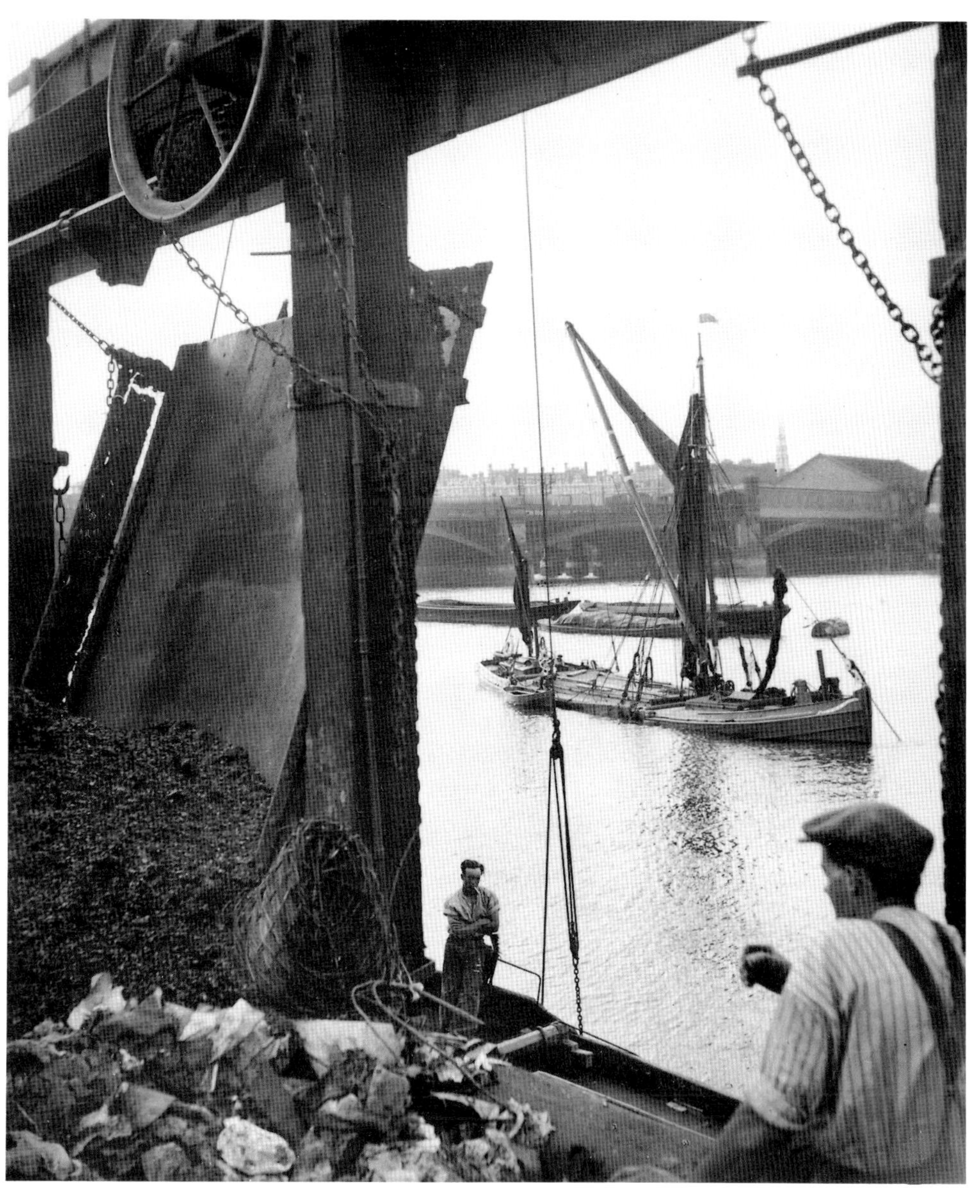

A view through Southwark Corporation's rubbish chutes at Greenmoor Wharf, Bankside, looking towards Blackfriars Railway Bridge (1886). A fully laden sailing barge is anchored, awaiting the tide for her journey downriver.

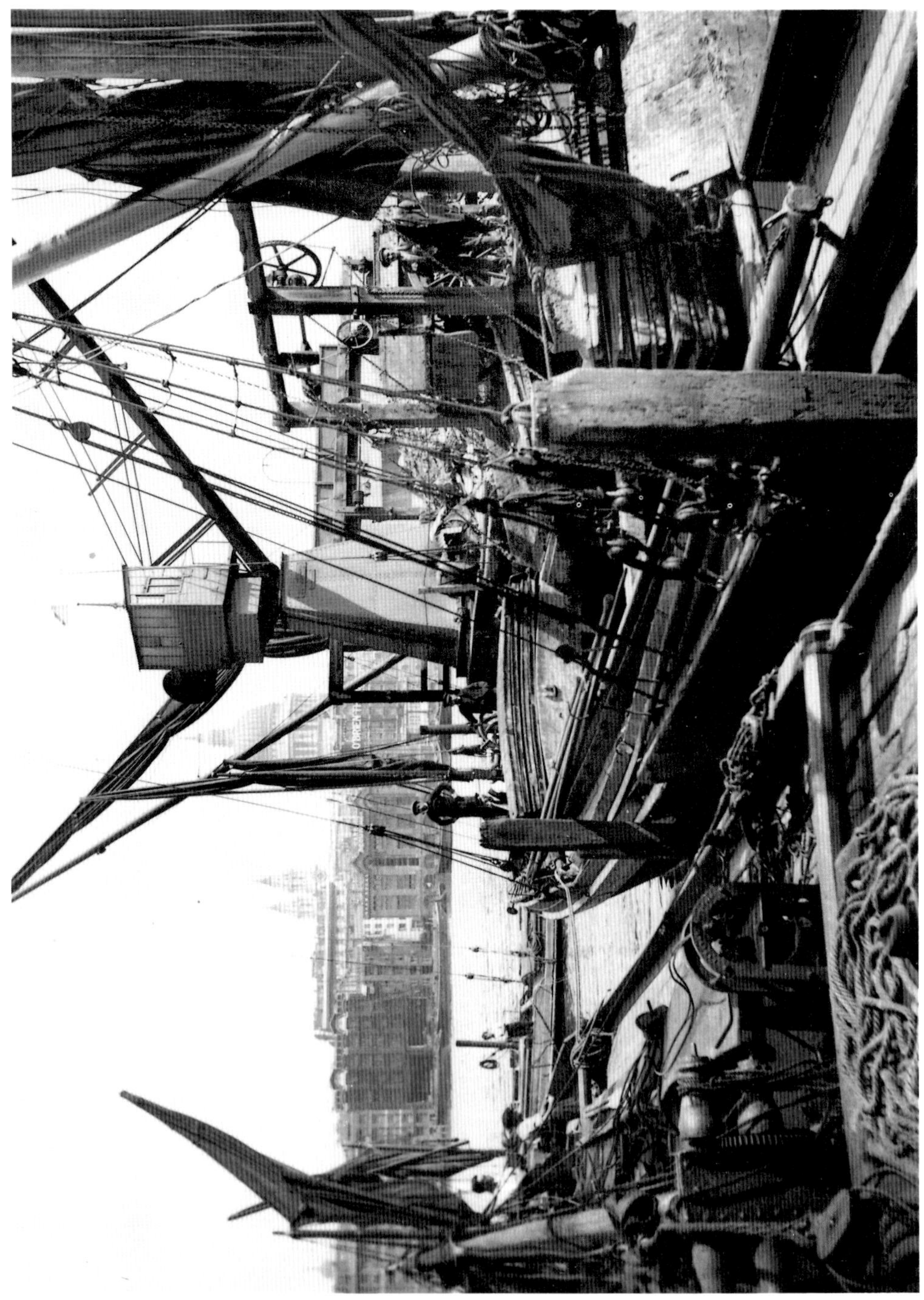

Sailing barges lying alongside Southwark Corporation's Greenmoor Wharf. The maze of rigging, masts, spars and sails of the barges, together with a hydraulic crane and St Paul's Cathedral, complete the skyline.

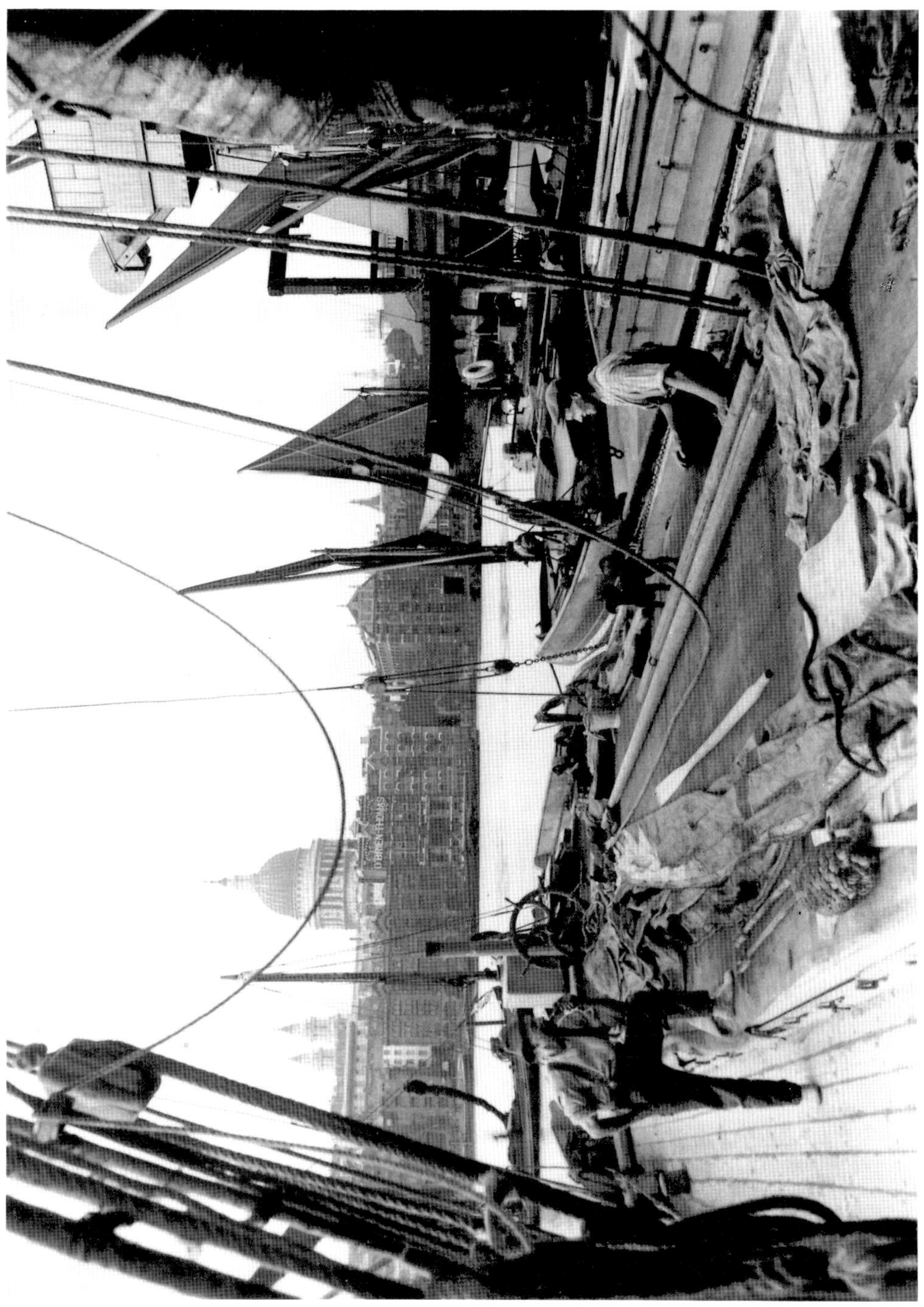

The skipper and mate of a sailing barge relax at Greenmoor Wharf. Once loaded with refuse, the barge will head downriver to the estuary. While most rubbish was used for land reclamation, in Kent and Essex, horse manure was separated out and used to fertilise agricultural land.

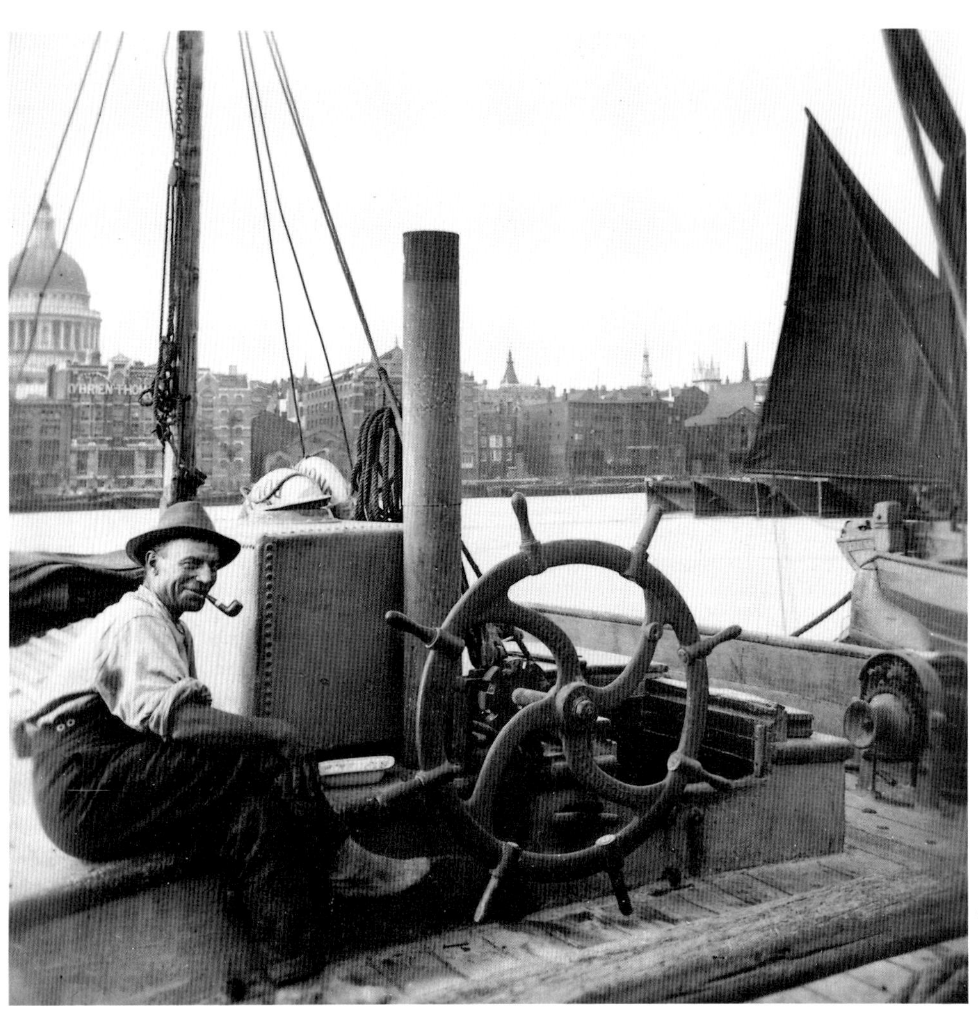

The sailing barge skipper, with pipe in mouth, takes it easy, in stockinged feet. The cast-iron, ›chaff-cutter‹, wheel is strictly utilitarian, as are the stove-chimney and the galvanised fresh water tank.

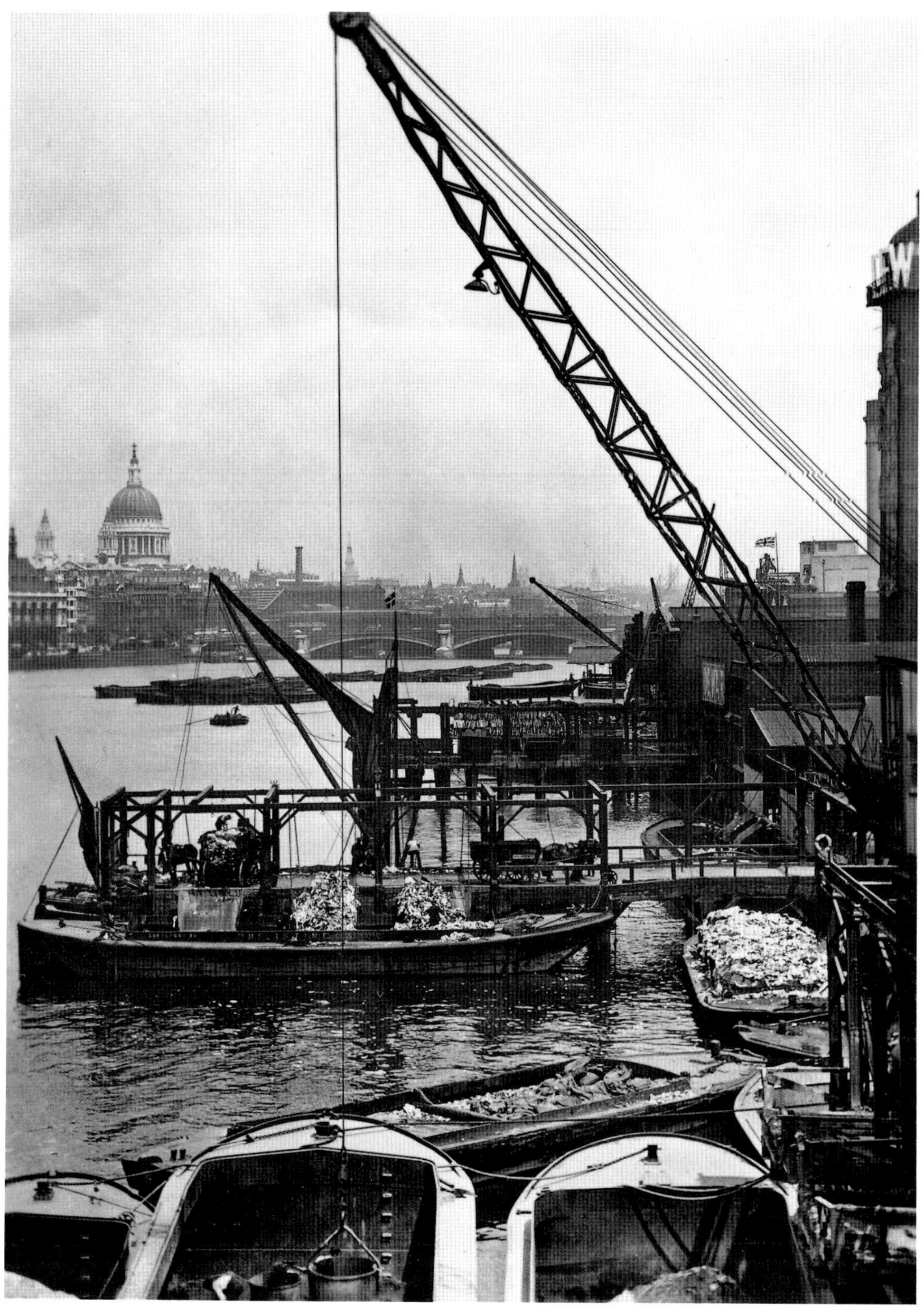

The Lambeth waterfront, east of Waterloo Bridge, was very active. The large crane is discharging sand and gravel, from lighters, at Baltic Wharf. Beyond is the jetty of the City Corporation's refuse depot at Letts Wharf. Rubbish is being shot directly from carts into a lighter and a sailing barge.

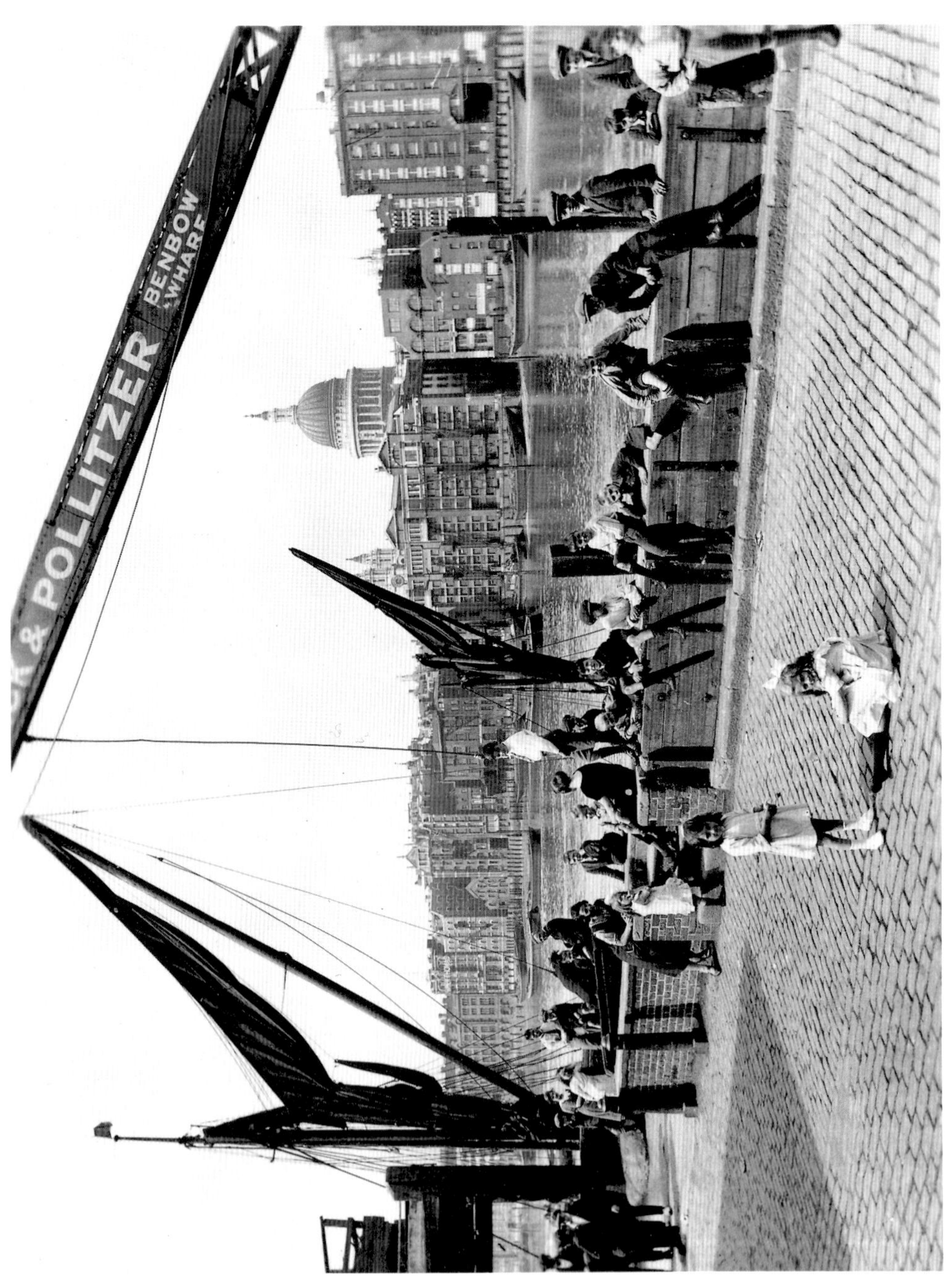

View of Bankside, by Beck and Pollitzer's Benbow Wharf, looking over to the late-nineteenth century City waterfront, west of Southwark Bridge. The ›Bank‹, as it was affectionately known, offered the children of local river workers endless entertainment.

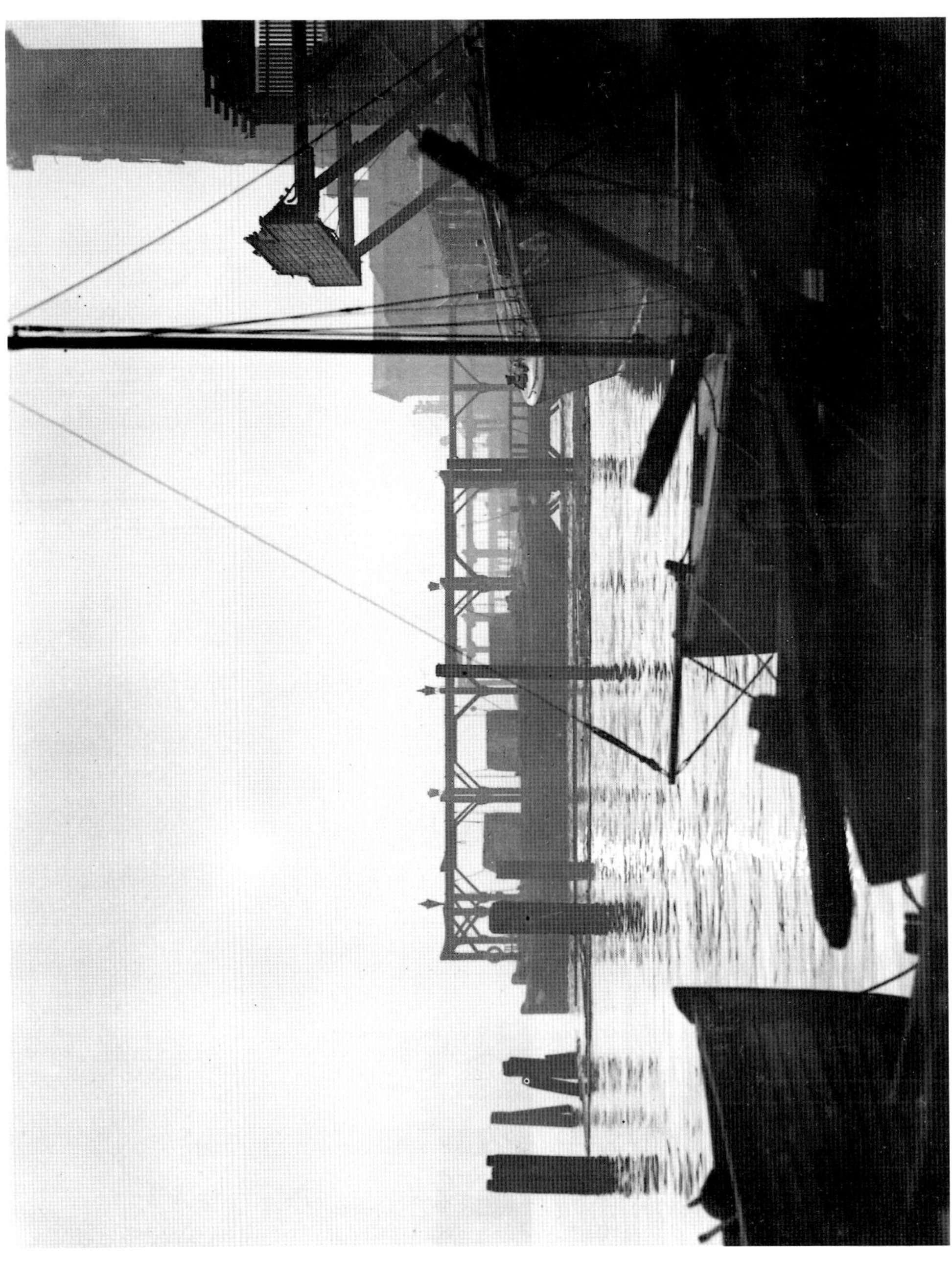

Sunrise over the Lambeth waterfront, looking east. In the early morning and at sunset the river took on a romantic, almost abstract, quality. The large tower, on the right, part of Dewar's Whisky Wharf, was built as a shot tower in 1789.

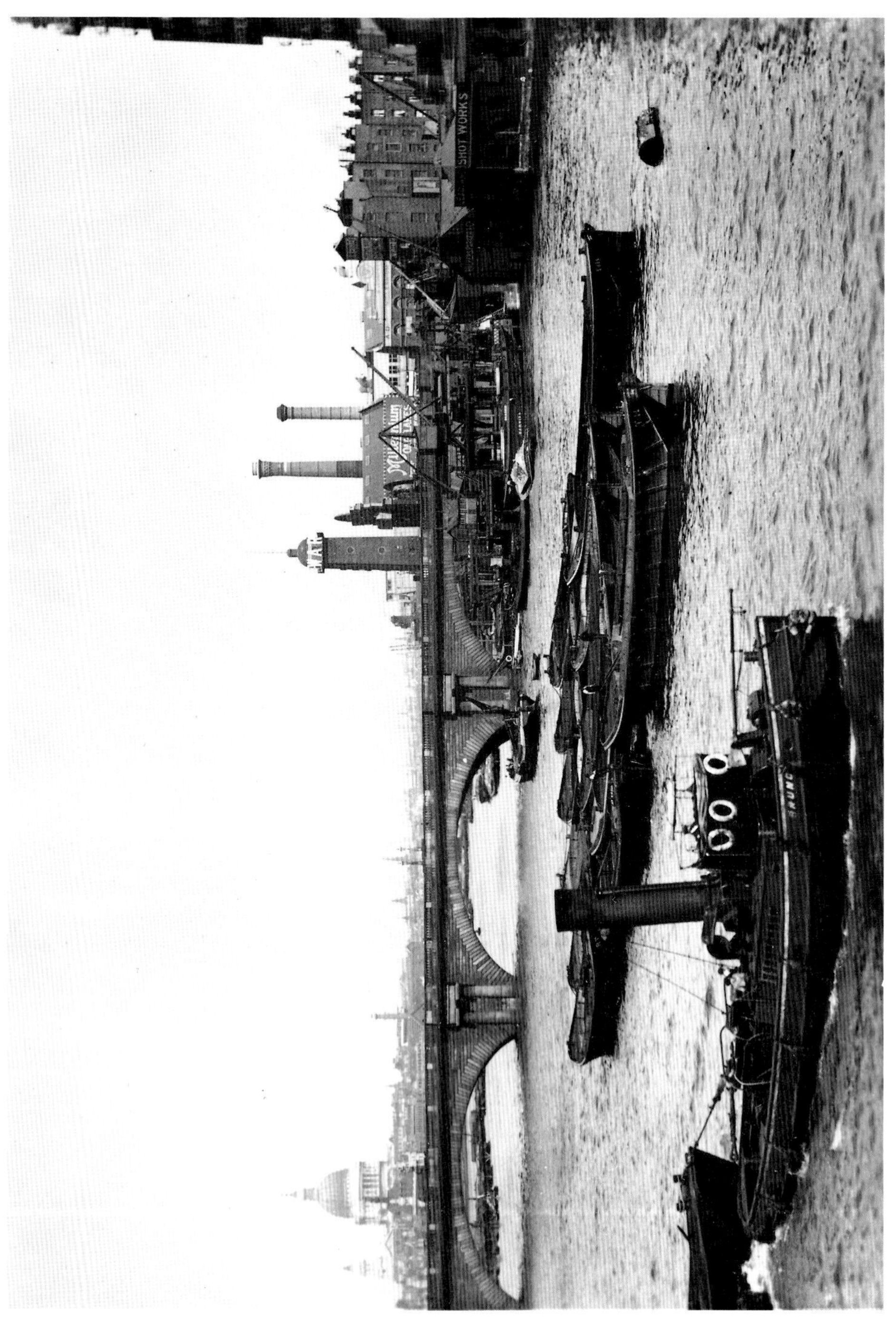

Old Waterloo Bridge (1817–1937) and the Lambeth waterfront. The shot tower of the Lambeth Lead Works appears on the extreme right and, beside it, jetties with cranes and derricks. Beyond the bridge can be seen Spiller's Millenium Mill. Empty lighters are moored at the Waterloo Barge Roads and the steam tug ›*Bruno*‹ can be seen with a tow.

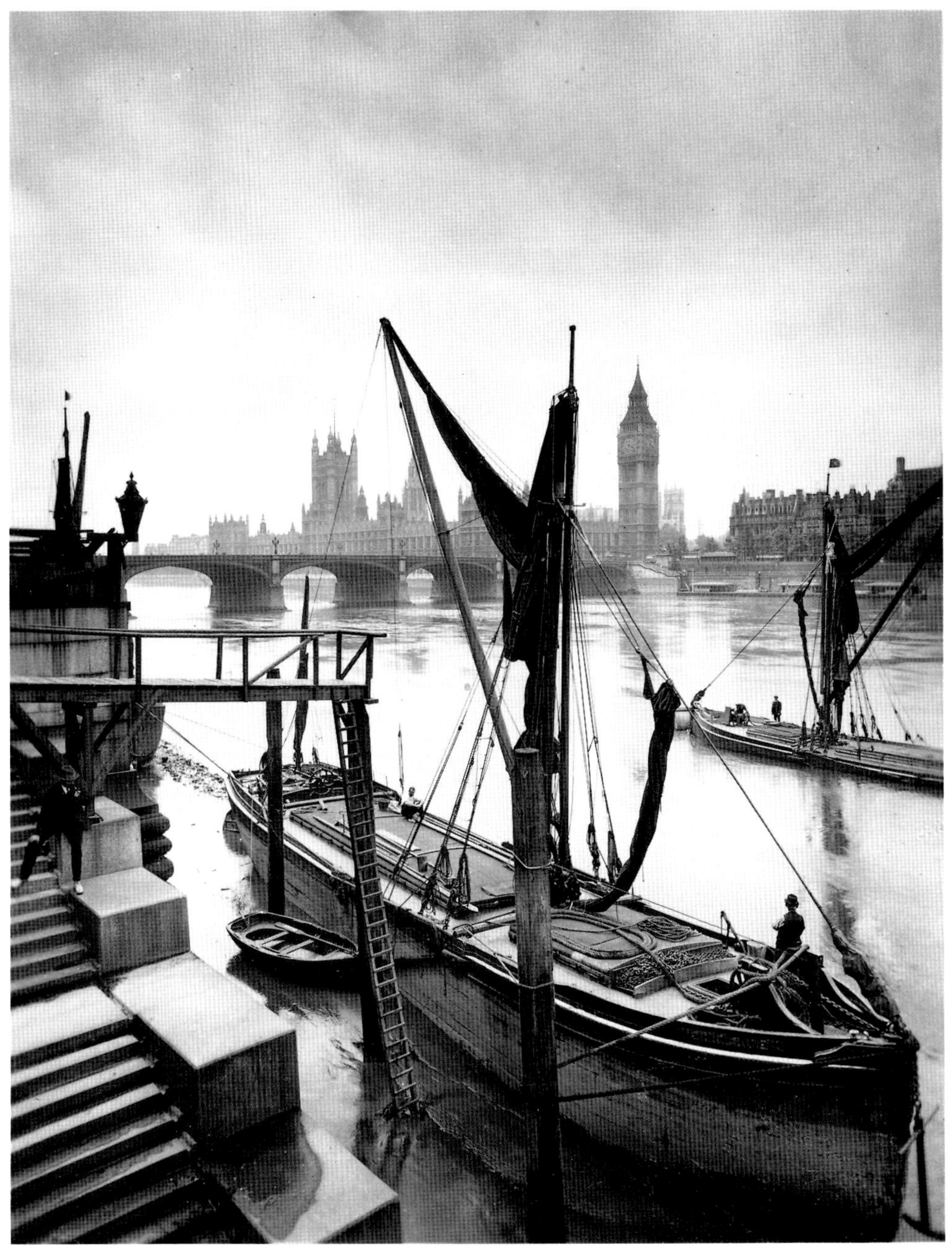

The Houses of Parliament (completed 1860) and Westminster Bridge (1862), seen from the stairs at County Hall, the headquarters of the London County Council. County Hall and its Embankment were completed in stages between 1922–1933 and the sailing barge, ›*Lizzie*‹, has probably offloaded building materials.

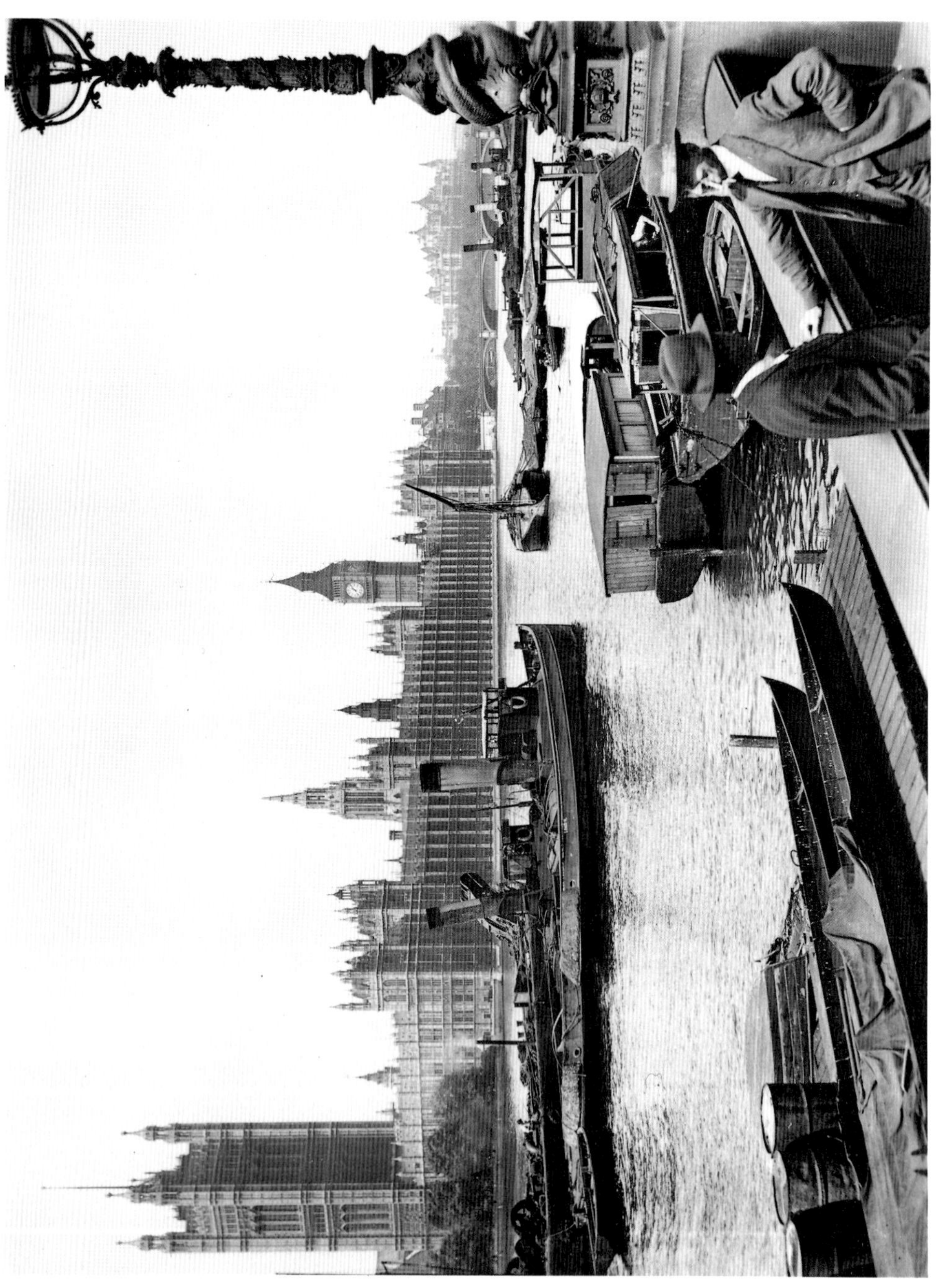

The Houses of Parliament, photographed from the eastern side of Lambeth Pier. Steam tugs, a salvage vessel, a sailing barge, coal barges and small craft, including a variety of skiffs, complete this busy scene.

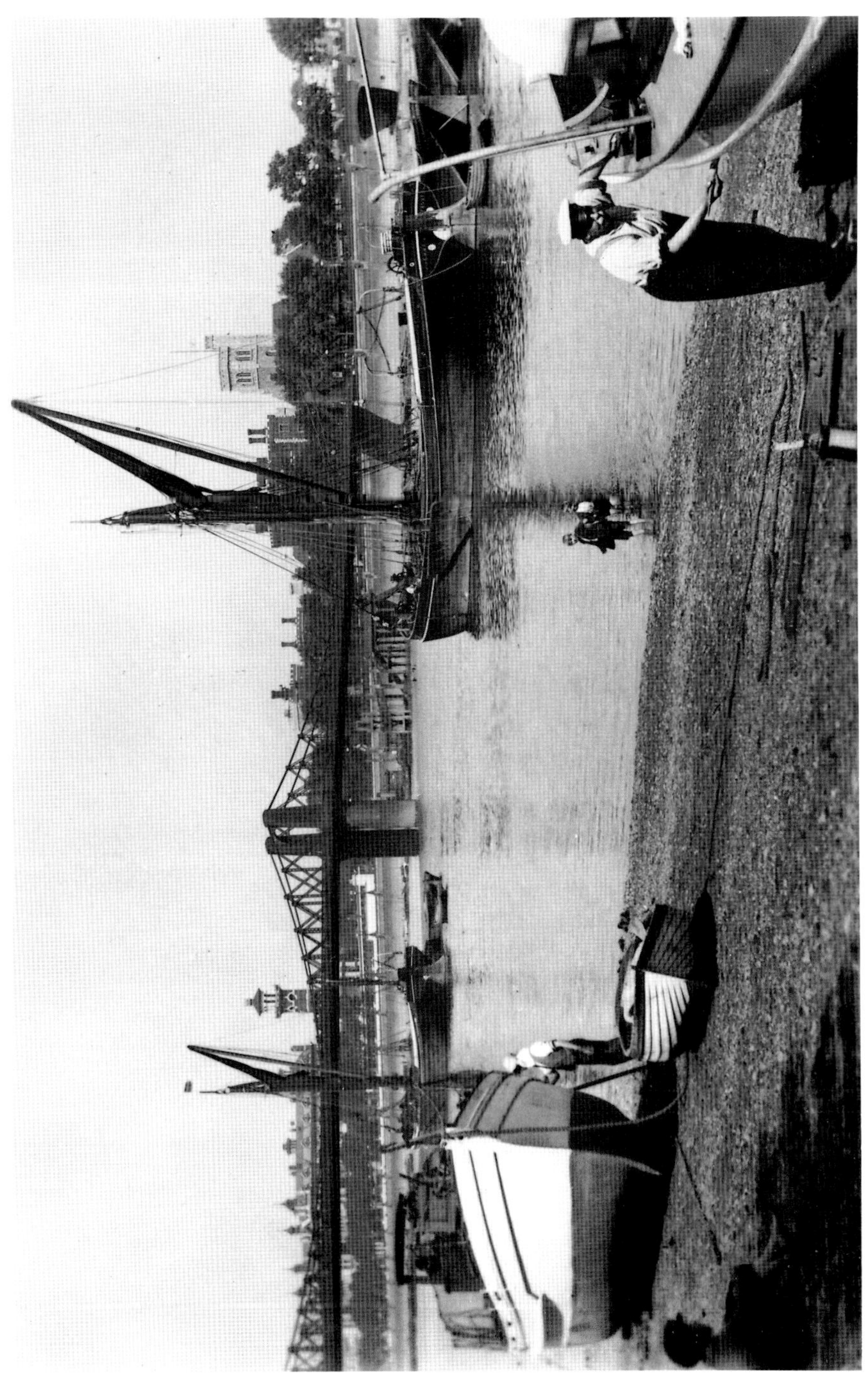

Old Lambeth Bridge (1862–1929), Lambeth Palace, and the Albert Embankment provide the background to this photograph taken from the foreshore at Horseferry Stairs. Sailing barges and lighters are moored in the channel, whilst boatowners and local children are taking advantage of the low tide for different sorts of amusement.

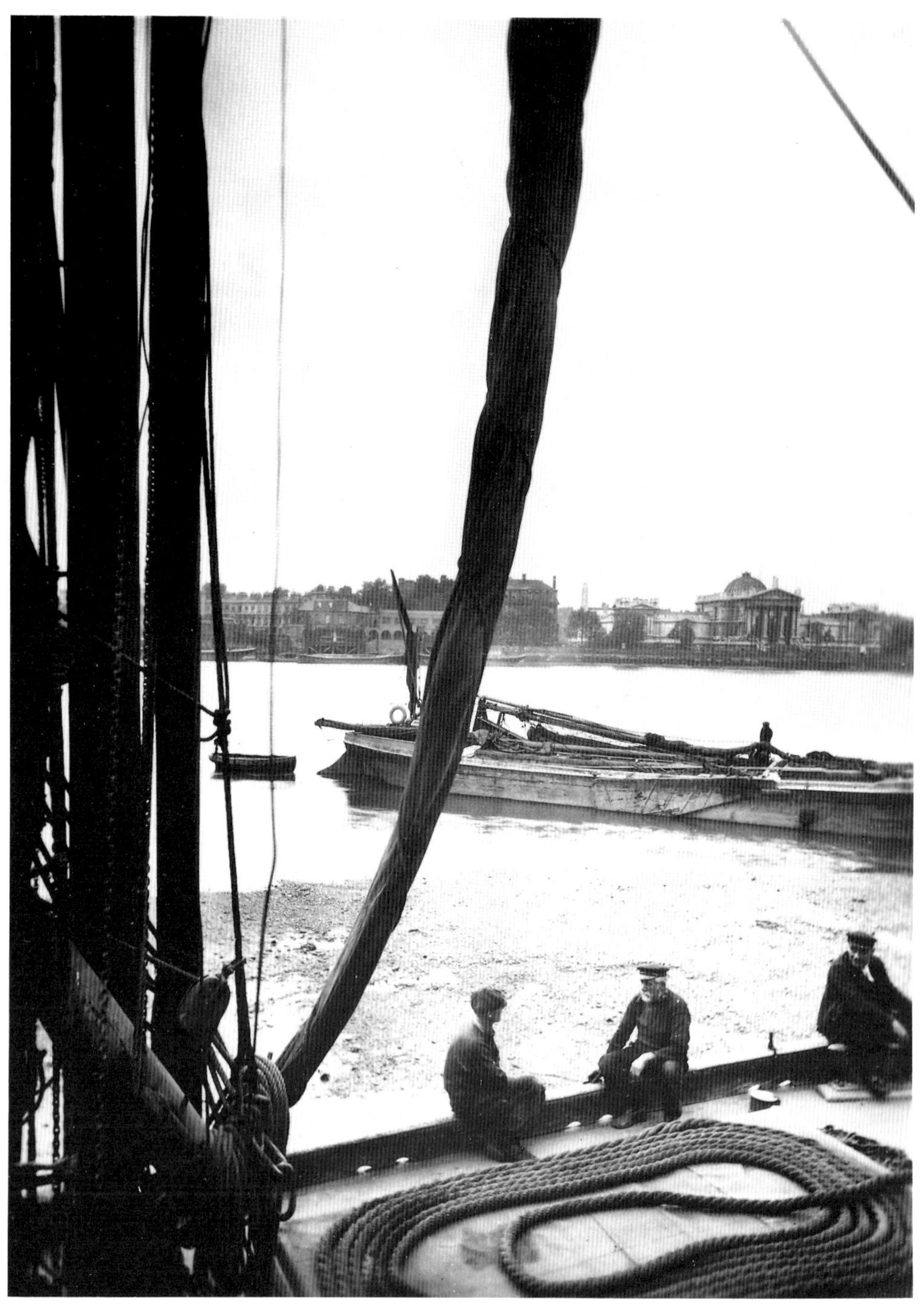

View towards Millbank and the Tate Gallery, from the Vauxhall foreshore. The sailing barges are probably lying of Brown's Flour Mills, one of eight working wharves immediately to the east of Vauxhall Bridge.

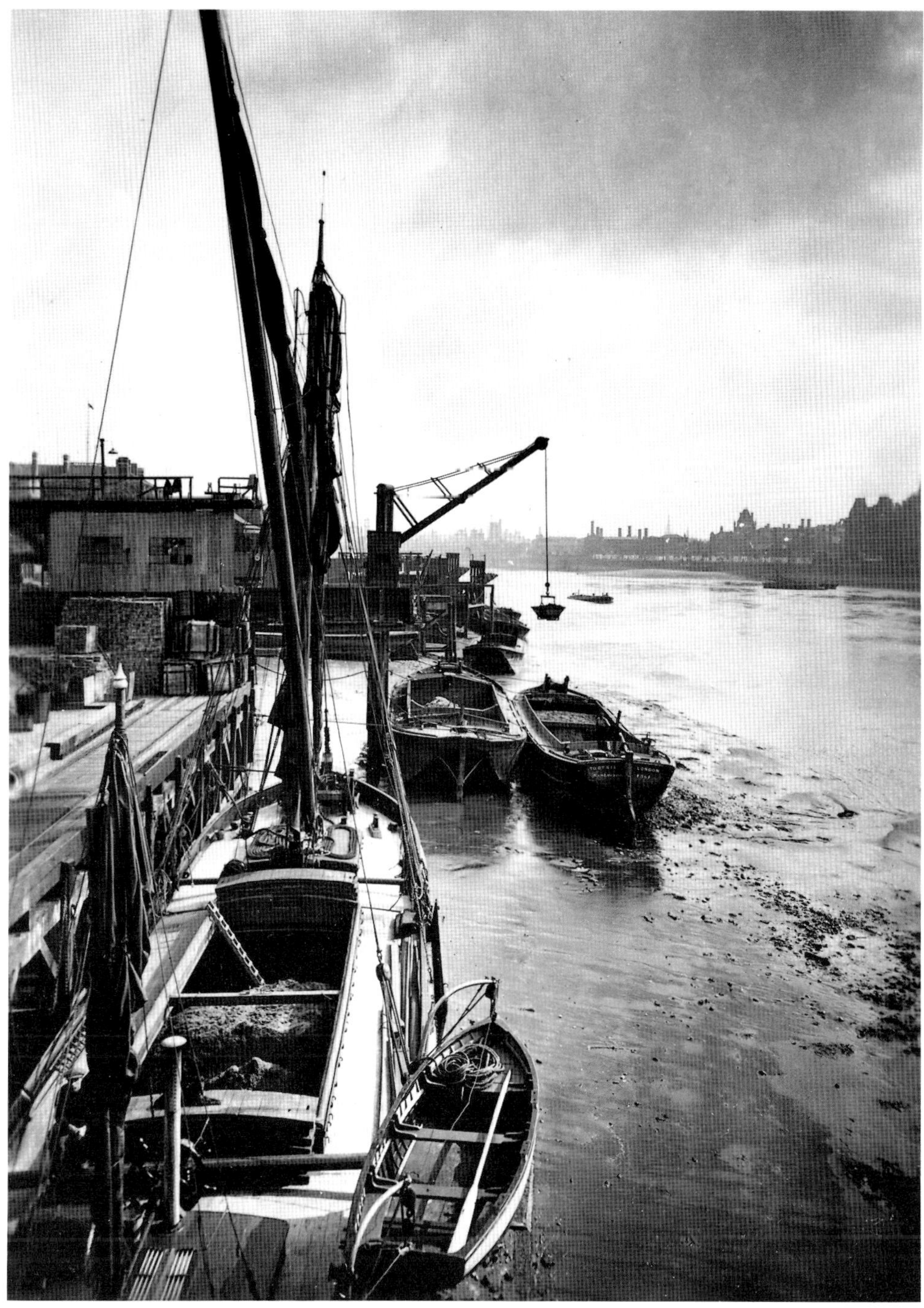

Grosvenor Road wharves, looking east, from the north side of Vauxhall Bridge. The sailing barge has brought building materials to Bridge Wharf. Beyond, a pillar hydraulic crane is discharging gravel from the ›*Tootsie*‹ – a tiller steered wooden dumb barge – and a lighter, at the Ham Grit Company's Wharf.

George Reid
Streets of London in the Twenties & Thirties
Edited by Mike Seaborne
THE PHOTO-LIBRARY II, 32 pages, 30 pictures, £ 2.95

Arthur Cross/Fred Tibbs
The London Blitz
Edited by Mike Seaborne
THE PHOTO-LIBRARY III, 32 pages, 30 pictures, £ 2.95

George Rodger
Magnum Opus
Fifty Years in Photojournalism
Edited by Colin Osman
112 pages, 100 pictures, duotone printing, £ 12.95 (softcover), £ 19.95 (hardcover)

Edith Tudor Hart
The Eye of Conscience
THE PHOTO-POCKET-BOOK I, 128 pages, 115 pictures, £ 5.95

Peter Keetman
A week at the Volkswagen factory
Pictures from 1953
Edited by Rolf Sachsse
THE PHOTO-POCKET-BOOK II, 96 pages, 75 pictures, duotone printing, £ 5.95

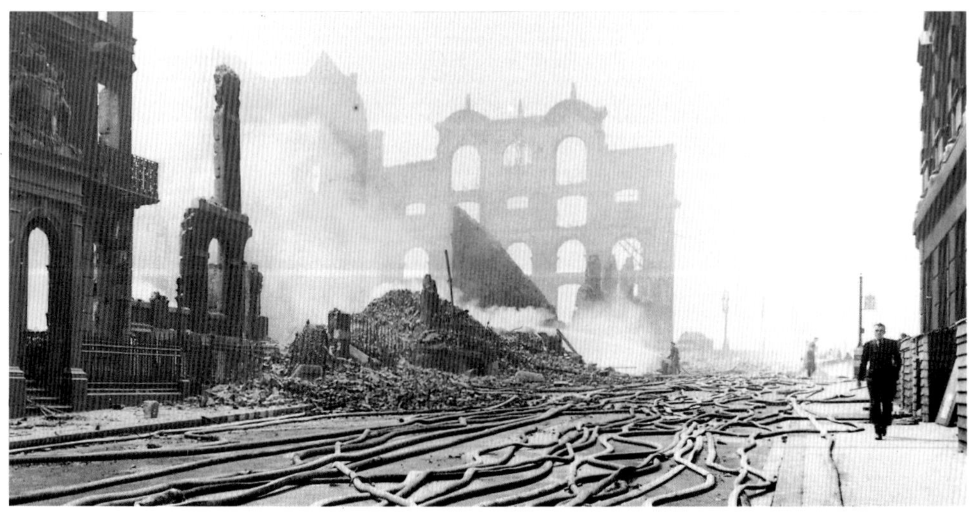

Dirk Nishen Publishing
19 Doughty Street, GB – London WC1N 2PT, 01/2420185